African Americans
— OF —
CENTRAL NEW JERSEY

African Americans

OF

CENTRAL NEW JERSEY

A History of Harmony and Hostility

BEVERLY MILLS AND ELAINE BUCK

THE
History
PRESS

Published by The History Press
Charleston, SC
www.historypress.com

First published 2023

Manufactured in the United States

ISBN 9781467154413

Library of Congress Control Number: 2023932169

Notice: The information in this book is true and complete to the best of our knowledge. It is offered without guarantee on the part of the authors or The History Press. The authors and The History Press disclaim all liability in connection with the use of this book.

*We dedicate this book to our husbands, Robert Mills and John B. Buck;
as well as the Mills children, Jason and Drew;
and grandchildren, Charde, Aviel, Hayden, Jameson, Megan and Zemhi*

*The Buck family children, Aaron, Jason and Shaniqua Jenkins Kennedy
Forever in Elaine's memory are her grandparents Robert and Queen Hester
Coleman and son Joseph (JB) Buck (1979–2000)*

*Beverly and Elaine would also like to extend a special thank-you to Patricia
True-Payne for her unwavering support of our work*

CONTENTS

FOREWORD

Local stories and the "power of place" are key to connecting people with history.[1] Weaving together the archival past with responses from today's community of the Sourland Mountain region of New Jersey, *Harmony and Hostility* exemplifies this connection. Authors Elaine Buck and Beverly Mills open an expanded prospect on New Jersey history by engaging with generations of families, Black and White, who have shaped the area throughout more than four centuries. Following on their first publication, *If These Stones Could Talk*, they have once again produced a work that beckons readers to envision the farms, fields, churchyards, graveyards and houses of their native community. Together, these two accessible, engaging books are major contributions in the efforts to broaden our understanding of the state's past.

If These Stones Could Talk introduced readers to the region's Black progenitors from the colonial era to the twentieth century. Buck and Mills, two creative and energetic women deeply engaged in civic and religious associations, were not initially historians. Yet the authors pulled at threads in archives, scoured local histories, tapped family genealogies and coaxed oral testimony to reveal and construct the presence and contributions of the locality's Black population. The frustrations of tracing men and women who were enslaved, Black, poor, without property, without political rights and barred from education did not discourage them from producing a second book-length work. *Harmony and Hostility* expands on their first account to examine the intertwining of Black and White lives in the region they call home. A telephone call from a White resident indignant that a Black burial ground might be eviscerated to lay a private driveway sent the pair down the path culminating in *If These Stones Could Talk*. Since its publication, descendants of both Whites and Blacks, living locally and far afield, have recognized their families in the book's stories. White descendants, struck that their ancestors had enhanced their wealth by the labor of the slaves they had owned, reached out to Buck and Mills. Reflecting on what they did not know, and why they did not know it, White residents and descendants of the region's families are coming to terms with a racialized and unequal past. *Harmony and Hostility* grew out of those responses Sourland Mountain stories evoked.

The result, *African Americans of Central New Jersey: A History of Harmony and Hostility*, is a collaboration between not solely Buck and Mills but also between the authors and the numerous families tied to the area's history. This communal effort yields both revelation and contemplation about the historical record in the region and, by implication, our nation. The past revealed is not universally positive or sugarcoated. This history is complex and messy: simultaneously cooperative, exploitative, joyful, sporadically violent, defeating, demoralizing and uplifting. But in demanding readers "see our past," Buck and Mills appeal to our better natures and national ideals and urge us to "recast our future." *Harmony and Hostility* implores readers of all backgrounds, classes, races and genders to espouse our American past as "compatriots."

Families are front and center in this work and not solely as a strategy for research. From generation to generation, readers grasp their struggles and triumphs. We learn the surnames shared by Black and White families but rarely the experiences truly shared. Early White New Jersey families who inherited landed and "personal" assets—including enslaved people—bested Black residents for opportunities in education, wealth and status. Startling perhaps for readers is the persistence of slavery in the North decades after the American Revolution. New Jersey's slow emergence from slaveholding underscores the advantages propertied Whites enjoyed. Throughout the nineteenth century, the Black minority of the region endeavored through fortitude and cohesiveness to gain and retain freedom and economic security. Their own churches were and remain central to their success. Harmony was undergirded at times (and continues to be undergirded) by ecumenical interracial cooperation. In the late nineteenth century, a number of Blacks struggled to gain middle-class respectability. Some rose to be respected employees in the service of White households or businesses. Husbands and wives rallied to secure plots of land and houses with comforts. They fostered community through churches, clubs and informal networks of support, especially for children. But gaining secure middle-class footholds, valued white-collar positions and access to education was a constant struggle. Even recognition for war service, as Buck and Mills show, did little to guarantee veterans the full benefits of having defended the nation.

The history the authors reveal of Blacks in the Sourland Mountain region is now no longer hiding in plain sight. Its fraught and complicated nature will spark reflection. Do we continue to inhabit separate worlds, perhaps more so than in the early nineteenth century? Are we still "Two Blocks Away, but Worlds Apart"? *Harmony and Hostility* will inspire readers to recognize the presence of the past and consider our own roles in shaping an inclusive national future.[2]

Donna J. Rilling
Department of History,
State University of New York at Stony Brook
August 2022

ACKNOWLEDGEMENTS

A special thank-you to Patricia True-Payne, who has continually been our rock, cheerleader and voice of reason. Your dedication and enthusiasm to this project have been unwavering, and we are grateful beyond measure.

We also thank Emma Lapsansky-Werner, PhD, who guided us with a firm, steady, nurturing hand from the beginning of this book to the closing page. We are grateful to Emma for sharing her astute knowledge of history, which inspired us to do our best in telling the story of this region's complicated past and its connection to the present.

We also would like to acknowledge those families and individuals who bravely made the decision to share their stories and bring them from the shadows into the light. Through your voices you bring us closer to understanding how we, Black and White people, can begin healing from an unequal and problematic past so we no longer navigate in separate worlds.

INTRODUCTION

Much of what is described as "national" historical events should really be seen as a patchwork of *local* events, intertwined and interacting with each other to produce a large—but often out of focus—narrative of "how we got here." The Sourland Mountains story is a stellar example of how race, class, ethnicity, gender, natural resources (e.g., quarries, fertile soil, access to river travel, climate and many other aspects of life) interact to produce a "culture." Others may argue that "big events"—such as wars, earthquakes, famines and powerful people versus the powerless—create the fabric of history. But the Sourland story provides an alternative perspective on the human story.

In our first book, *If These Stones Could Talk*, we began by asking questions: Who walked before us in our little community? What happened in their lives, and how can we tell their stories? How can their stories help us untangle the complicated American story? Our decision to start with cemeteries and the stories they tell set the stage for us to draw back the curtain to tell the story of a community that is taking control of its past, its present and future.

In this sequel, we invite our readers to return with us to where the African American presence in the Sourland Mountain and surrounding regions of New Jersey connects to the earliest days of America. We will bring to light more voices from both Black and White inhabitants in a region where race has distorted the stories of both Black and White builders. We bring Black people to the forefront, because if it were not for the enslaved and freed

African Americans, the flourishing economic landscape would look vastly different. The free labor of Black bodies enabled White bodies not only to grow but also to thrive to partake in the American dream, a dream based on the premise that one segment of society was inherently more entitled than others. How does a community become the place where Black people sink roots in soil, build homes in which to raise families and establish a church with a shepherd to lead their flock to provide them with the tools to navigate a Christian life in an unforgiving world? This book looks at how—once able to safely congregate away from the mistrustful eyes of White people—the Black church offered a healing balm to spirits continually broken and torn asunder. How does a community blossom from a group of people who started out as someone's possession but persevered to boldly claim their rights to be part of this American dream? Our story highlights the African American experience. But this book does not look at the region through only a Black lens. We look to tell the stories through the eyes of some of the region's White families as well, as both groups have grappled with the distortions of America's racial legacies, legacies that reflect the intermingling of past and present pain for surprising numbers of Americans, even as those legacies reflect deep roots and enduring institutions, long-standing friendships and admirable community stability.

In this new narrative we dig deeper to explore the economy, land use and cultural patterns, as well as memories and historical research that underpin those stories. Interweaving personal stories lived and/or remembered, we examine some of the building blocks of a region and of American racial complexity. History is often told in sweeping generalizations and in linear storylines, but it's actually *lived* through the granular and meandering narratives of human cooperation and exploitation, human kindness and human hate—human generosity and human greed—and these phenomena are often intertwined in complex ways. Also in these pages, we point to some of the ways forward if the Sourland Mountain communities—and indeed all American communities—are to build toward the aspirations of those who built the nation. This combination of Indigenous, European, Asian, South American and African people stumbled along as the nation was growing but in the twenty-first century might avail themselves of a path forward that honors the gifts and aspirations—and acknowledges the harm—of America's centuries-long path to getting "here." This book—built on evidence drawn from scholarly publications, popular history sources, newspapers, census records, land records, church archives, oral histories and personal interviews—is an invitation to our compatriots to join us in our mission to chart a path forward that, in the words of a twenty-first-century president, "builds back better."

The story of New Jersey's Sourland Mountain region—one of the nation's wealthiest—is analogous to stories all across America. Coal and iron, oil and wheat, oranges and tobacco, livestock and cars and textiles and technological ingenuity, along with fertile land and human stamina and bravery have developed America into one of the wealthiest and most politically powerful nations in the world. The dark side of that growth is exploitation, racial injustice, greed and violence—and more than a little dishonesty about who we Americans are as a people. Using verbal "snapshots" of people, places and events, our narrative aims to help us, in New Jersey, to see our past and recast our future—and to inspire others—region by region to undertake a similar hard look and honest reckoning with their own regions. Toward that end, *Harmony and Hostility* aims to pave a path to healing, by giving life and specificity to some of the myriad people, events and memories—representing many backgrounds, experiences and perspectives—who helped to shape the Sourland Mountain region's life and culture.

The chapters of this book shuttle back and forth through time, reflecting the vacillating intersections between events and perspectives of the past, present and the aspirational/possible futures. Though our book is somewhat framed within formal scholarly boundaries, it is also a collage of personal perspectives on historical events and perspectives, which we hope will help us and our compatriots to embrace a more humane, responsible, compassionate and empathic future.

A WORD ABOUT LABELS

In this work, we refer to people by several different terms because we believe that no single word really describes who people are. The label "White" has come to be synonymous with people of European descent—and the quality of "Whiteness" has come to have meanings far beyond color or nationality. "White" in America is associated with dominance and privilege, while the terms "Black" or "of color" or "African American" often conjure up notions of "lower class."

While we recognize that these labels have been invented by the dominant caste to be used to exclude "others" by using physical features to gauge Whiteness, we also recognize that in America many have lost sight of the fact that White and Black are sociopolitical terms, used mainly to create divisiveness and unrest.

Nevertheless, as we wrestled with these terms, we decided to keep it simple and use the shortened labels of "White" and "Black" as we share the stories and history of the people we introduce in this book.

All our best,

Beverly and Elaine

FOUNDING WHITE AND BLACK FAMILIES OF THE SOURLAND MOUNTAIN REGION AND SURROUNDING AREA

THE WHITE BLACKWELL FAMILY

Robert Blackwell Sr. (1643–1717)
First Blackwell to settle in the colonies; former husband of Ann Blackwell; husband of Mary Manningham Blackwell

Robert Blackwell Jr. (1673–1757)
First Blackwell to settle in New Jersey; son of Robert and Ann Blackwell; husband of Elizabeth Combs Blackwell

Thomas Blackwell (1714–1777)
Son of Robert Jr. and Elizabeth C. Blackwell; husband of Susannah Titus Blackwell

Andrew Blackwell (1750–1818)
Great-grandson of Robert Sr. and Mary M. Blackwell; grandson of Robert Jr. and Elizabeth C. Blackwell; son of Thomas and Susannah T. Blackwell, owner of Frost Blackwell

The Black Blackwell Family

Frost Blackwell (c. 1786–death date unknown)
Parents unknown; property of Andrew Blackwell; freed in 1819

Nancy Vanvactor Blackwell (c. 1794–1882)
Parents unknown; wife and property of Frost Blackwell; purchased in 1827 by her husband, Frost

Samuel Blackwell (1817–1907)
Oldest son of Frost and Nancy V. Blackwell

Nancy E. Blackwell (1841–1919)
Granddaughter of Frost and Nancy V. Blackwell; daughter of Samuel and Maxmilla Light Blackwell; wife of Joseph W. Smith Sr.

George Blackwell (1856–1940)
Grandson of Frost and Nancy V. Blackwell; son of Samuel and Maxmilla Light Blackwell; husband of Sarah R. Blackwell

The White Hart Family

Reverend Oliver Hart (1723–1795)
Pastor of the First Baptist Church of Charleston, South Carolina (1750–1780); pastor of the Old School Baptist Church, Hopewell, New Jersey (1780–1795); owner of Friday Truehart

The Black Truehart Family

Friday Truehart (1767–1843)
Property of Reverend Oliver Hart; son of Dinah (property of Reverend Oliver Hart); husband of Judah Shue

Judah (Juda) Shue Truehart (1773–1855)
Property and wife of Friday Truehart

Isaac Truehart (1792–1886)
Oldest son of Friday and Judah Truehart; husband of Martha

William H. Truehart (1845–1932)
Son of Isaac and Martha Truehart; grandson of Friday and Judah Truehart

THE WHITE BLEW FAMILY

Michael Blew Sr. (c. 1704–1786)
Settled in Somerset County circa 1740; husband of Elinor "Nelly" Hollinsett; owner of Thomas, Judith and Moses Blew and other enslaved individuals

THE BLACK BLEW FAMILY

Thomas Blew (dates unknown)
Parents unknown; property of Michael and Elinor Blew; husband of Judith Blew

Judith (Juda) Blew (1763–1857)
Parents unknown; property of Michael and Elinor Blew; wife of Thomas Blew

Moses Blew (1786–1874)
Property of Michael and Elinor Blew; son of Judith and Thomas Blew

THE BLACK SMITH FAMILY

Joseph B. Smith (1818–1890)
No records uncovered prior to Joseph B. Smith; husband of Jane

Joseph W. Smith Sr. (1851–1909)
Son of Joseph B. and Jane Smith; husband of Nancy Blackwell Smith

Joseph W. Smith Jr. (1877–1956)
Son of Joseph W. and Nancy B. Smith; husband of Cora Houston Smith

Alfonso P. Smith (1898–1986)
Great-great-grandson of Frost and Nancy Blackwell; great-grandson of Samuel and Maximilla Blackwell; grandson of Joseph W. Sr. and Nancy Blackwell; son of Joseph W. Jr. and Cora H. Smith; husband of Clara B. Clark Smith

Clara B. Clark Smith (1902–1961)
Daughter of Ballard and Pinky Clark; wife of Alfonso P. Smith

BLACK IMMIGRANTS FROM VIRGINIA TO NEW JERSEY

Henry Ballard Clark (1874–1955)
Husband of Pinky Coles Clark; migrated from Gretna, Virginia, to New Jersey at the end of nineteenth century

Pinky Coles Clark (1874–1963)
Wife of Henry Ballard Clark, migrated from Chatham, Virginia, to New Jersey at the end of the nineteenth century

William Mobile Ashby (1890–1991)
Born in Carter's Grove, Virginia; husband of Mary Arnold of Hopewell, New Jersey

PART I

BONDAGE, FREEDOM AND THE BUILDING OF EARLY WHITE AND BLACK COMMUNITIES

1

WHITE AND BLACK COMMUNITIES
GROW SIDE BY SIDE BUT
NOT TOGETHER

In 1824, after touring for seven weeks, Peter Chandler, a White Connecticut businessman, traveled through New Jersey. After crossing the Delaware River into Pennsylvania, he described what he had seen: "Today left the land of slavery, New Jersey. The blacks are permitted to be held in bondage. Almost every farmer has from one to half a dozen slaves."[3]

In *A Study of Slavery in New Jersey* (1896), Henry Scofield Cooley, a late nineteenth-century historian, also remarked on the pervasiveness of slavery in the state: "The maximum slave population in New Jersey given by the U.S. Census Reports is 12,422 in the year 1800."[4] And although the slave population showed a decrease after the passage of New Jersey's Gradual Abolition Act of 1804, "at the beginning of the present [i.e. nineteenth] century, Cooley noted, New Jersey had a larger slave population than any other State north of Maryland, except New York."[5] Indeed, two full decades after the passing of the Gradual Abolition Act, New Jersey remained a society with a system where, as Cooley described it, "whites and blacks struggled to define slavery's end."[6]

Among the early nineteenth-century Black New Jersey residents Cooley described were a number of Hunterdon County families who shared surnames with the White families that had held them in bondage. Thus, the Black families whose lives we will highlight include families who have made their homes and lives in Hunterdon County for more than two centuries. A 1984 study listed more than 130 surnames of pre-nineteenth-century Sourland Mountain settlers and their descendants who lived in portions of Hunterdon County—which includes present-day Mercer County—and Somerset County.[7] These two counties encompass a central New Jersey region that included the Sourland Mountain area and had been home to a nineteenth-century population of Whites, free Blacks and enslaved Blacks, with surnames that linked all three constituencies. This copious listing of names includes such families as Blackwell, Boyer, Truehart, Grover, Hagaman, McIntire, Nevius, Peterson, Stives Raisner, Hubbard, Schenk, Smith, Waldron, Hunt and Van Lieu, which, in many cases, date back to eighteenth-century residents. However, though Black *and* White families shared the names, a slight spelling difference often separated the races. Nevertheless, similar surnames could be traced through manumission papers filed by Hunterdon and Somerset County slave owners as early as 1788—sixteen years prior to New Jersey's Gradual Abolition Act passed in 1804. What can we learn about the communities of the region by digging into the stories of these shared surnames and the early manumissions, in some cases, as well as cases of slavery and bondage enduring well into the mid-nineteenth century? In what ways were the lives of Black Hunterdon County residents intertwined with their neighbors of "other race"?

Cooley reported that though it took two legislative sessions, the manumission bill was eventually passed:

> *Every child born of a slave after the fourth of July of that year* [1804] *was to be free, but should remain the servant of the owner of the mother, as if bound out by the overseers of the poor, until the age of twenty-five, if a male, and twenty-one years, if a female. The right to the services of such negro child was perfectly clear and free. It was assignable or transferable. One person might be the owner of the mother and another have gained the right to the services of the child. Masters were compelled to file with the county clerk a certificate of the birth of every child of a slave. This certificate was kept for future evidence of the age of the child. The owner of the mother must maintain the child for one year; after that period he might, by giving due notice, abandon it. Every negro child thus abandoned, like other poor children, was to be regarded as a pauper of the township or county, and be bound out to services by overseers of the poor. This provision, allowing masters to refuse to maintain children born to their slaves, was the source of considerable fraud upon the treasury, and was the cause of many supplements and amendments to the law of 1804 in succeeding years.*[8]

The transition from slavery to abolition was clearly a contentious one. Nevertheless, between 1787 and 1856, more than five hundred manumissions were recorded in Hunterdon County, listing the name of the slaveholder, the enslaved person and the location of the slave owner's home. These lists of slave owners' surnames have proven to be a key resource for Black descendants' efforts to trace their ancestors' history through court manumission and census records. For many African Americans, however, manumission and abolition left them only a broken trail to pursue questions such as who were our people—our ancestors—and where did we come from? Could such questions be answered beyond oral histories and anecdotes passed down throughout the generations? How to locate clues to centuries-old questions—questions that started with over twelve million bodies plucked like ripe berries from the African continent? How would it be possible to identify forebearers who were shackled and packed into the holds of disease-ridden slave ships that were riddled with despair? How does one identify which floating vessel of horror carried their ancestors to the unspeakable fate that awaited them?

William Blake's *The History of Slavery and the Slave Trade*, published in 1861, is one place to start. In this narrative, Blake recorded firsthand accounts of seamen, captains, businessmen and doctors who described what they witnessed on various slave ships during the Middle Passage. One alleged eyewitness, Dr. Trotter, recounted,

> *They had not so much room as a man in his coffin, either in length or breadth. It was impossible for them to turn or shift with any degree of ease. In the interval of being upon deck they are fed twice. They also have a pint of water allowed to each of them a day, which being divided is served out of them at two different times, namely, after their meals. The meals consist of rice, yams, and horse-beans, with now and then a little beef and bread. After meals they are made to jump in their irons. This is called dancing by the slave-dealers. In every ship he (the ship Captain) has been desired to flog such as would not jump. He had generally a cat-of-nine-tails in his hand among the women, and the chief mate, he believes, another among the men. When the scuttles are obliged to be shut, the gratings are not sufficient for airing the rooms. He never himself could breathe freely, unless immediately under the hatchway.*[9]

American history-telling has not included much about the Middle Passage and its unspeakable horrors. Difficult discussions involving the Middle

Passage and the African American story are relatively new additions to twenty-first-century school curricula, but as of the early twenty-first century, this narrative is under threat of being suppressed or removed from the "American" story. For over four hundred years, this story has remained in shadow, muted and now poised to be erased completely from the American history narrative in several states.

By the early seventeenth century, enslaved people had arrived in nearly all of the New World colonies, including the Dutch colony of New Jersey. And beginning in the 1660s, when New Jersey came under British control, the rate of slave imports grew steadily. Colonel Richard Morris of Shrewsbury had sixty or more slaves working his mill and plantation as early as 1680.[10] By 1776, "one-fifth of the residents of the thirteen colonies were shackled under the brutal slave system,"[11] with the number topping 12,000 in New Jersey, according to the 1800 U.S. census. More than 1,300 of these bound workers were in Hunterdon County, a geographical region that included White, free Black, enslaved Black and Indigenous people living "together" in communities but on diverging trajectories—as America grew to embrace the belief that some people were more entitled than others to power and privilege through the former's own contrived hierarchy. The belief system that underpinned inequality was apparent even in the early Christian churches where Black and White parishioners sometimes worshiped together. Thus, early town records such as the Old School Baptist Church in Hopewell designated Black members either by "a negro woman of," "negro man of," or Samuel a Black, Richard a Black or Judy a Black.[12]

But by the late eighteenth century, a new school of thought was developing, endorsed not only by elite and powerful White Americans but also by some Black leaders who sought more autonomy for their communities. Such community autonomy among Black communities was evidenced by Reverend Richard Allen and Absalom Jones, who spearheaded the formation of Philadelphia's Free African Society (1787)—a largely northern organization that provided social services to Black people when their White brethren failed to help individuals or families who were hurt or ill, orphaned or otherwise in difficulty. As early as the 1780s, "Free African" organizations sprang up in other regions—including Hopewell Township—as the ideas of Allen and Jones echoed across America and eventually around the world. Some free Black people pooled their resources to offer aid, including envisioning ways to return to Africa.[13] But although the founders of these organizations were men and women of the highest esteem, they did not escape White suspicion and resentment.[14] Richard Allen's founding of an independent Methodist church in the 1790s and Absalom Jones's simultaneous establishment of the African Episcopal Church constituted one response to the mistreatment of Black parishioners at Philadelphia's Old St. George's Methodist Church, which had abruptly required Black worshippers to worship in a separate section of the church from the White congregation.[15]

Out of Philadelphia's Free African Society grew Allen's new denomination—the African Methodist Episcopal Church—which became fully established in the same year as the ultra-separatist American Colonization Society (ACS). Founded in 1816 and led by Reverend Robert Finley, a White Presbyterian affiliated with the Princeton Theological Seminary, the ACS championed the idea that the presence of freed Black people was a threat to America's economic and social well-being—a potential cause of unrest among the enslaved. Thus, argued the ACS, free Black people should not only be required to worship in separate quarters but also be transported out of America to Africa, where they could realize their full potential in the "land of their fathers"—far away from where their very presence might foment insurrection among American slaves. Finley was one of a number of White settlers who shared this opinion, and the American Colonization Society quickly gained membership.[16]

Membership Certificate for the American Colonization Society. *Library of Congress.*

In the twenty-first century, Princeton University, looking backward to investigate its complicity in the historic institution of American slavery, commissioned a report titled *Princeton Seminary and Slavery.*[17] The report found that although the seminary itself had not owned slaves, its founders, including Ashbel Green, Samuel Miller, Archibald Alexander and Charles Hodge, had all used enslaved laborers even though they had expressed opposition to slavery "in principle." The ACS's position was that though the immediate emancipation of enslaved people was not economically feasible, people of African descent should gradually be "returned" to Africa. The twenty-first-century Princeton report expanded on the intertwining of morality, complicity, expediency, and economics:

> *Slavery was interwoven into the* [nineteenth-century] *American economy. Its presence was felt in the mills and workshops of New England as well as on the plantations in Georgia. It created the capital needed to build schools of higher education in Virginia as well as in New York. One did not have to own slaves to benefit from slavery. Yet it is not helpful for this type of study to paint everyone who simply participated in the economy in the same shade. Most people would agree that there is a difference between the owner of a cotton plantation in Georgia and someone who buys a cotton shirt in Boston. It is often difficult to talk about how. This report approaches the problem by viewing donors based on their relationship with slavery. These categories are far from perfect, and individuals often do not fit neatly into one, but they do provide a framework for discussing how a person could potentially benefit financially in a slave economy. The first is, of course, slave owners. The second is a person who does not personally own slaves, but was nevertheless raised in a family of slave owners and thus accrued financial advantages by extension. The third consists of individuals who profited from slavery through business and financial ties. Where the second category is determined by chance of birth, the third is voluntary and often deliberate. Finally, the fourth category is the cotton shirt buyer who benefited from slavery far down the production line. Ultimately, the Seminary sits in the middle of this spectrum. It benefited financially from those in its denominational family who owned slaves and who profited from the slave system. It also invested its funds in organizations that both profited from slavery and financed its expansion.*[18]

Thus, the 2018 Princeton report makes clear that by 1816, some White New Jersey dwellers were strategizing about how and when to send African

Americans out of the country that they had helped to build. Simultaneously, free Black followers of leaders like Richard Allen and Absalom Jones were developing their own communities by establishing churches in Philadelphia, New York, Delaware—and in Pennington, New Jersey—as followers of the newly formed African Methodist Episcopal Church. It is unclear how many African Americans endorsed the ACS plans (as Richard Allen had initially done) as a viable alternative to disenfranchisement in the United States. But there were certainly important differences between the goals of the ACS to remove free African Americans and the goal of African Americans—in other words, to end slavery. But Paul Cuffee, a wealthy Black New England shipowner and likely the wealthiest African American in the country, represented the position that Black people—free *and* enslaved—should be able to *choose* to relocate to Africa, where they could fulfill a potential that could not be found in America.[19] While Cuffee's interest in aiding both freed and enslaved Black people overlapped with a few White American "abolitionists," many other White Americans had no interest in interrupting the system of slavery, even though they sometimes worried about the potential threat of slave rebellions.[20]

For their part, most free Black people had little interest in African colonization. Having been born in the United States, they considered America their home, just as White people who had relocated to America did. Black Americans voiced a variety of other concerns, too. As one historian has summarized it: "Most free blacks realized that colonization would actually make it easier for slavery to continue in the United States rather than hastening its disappearance, as some supporters claimed."[21]

Prior to the formal establishment of his Philadelphia Mother Bethel AME Church, Richard Allen made his way into the Hopewell Valley region for an extended stay within the household of Jonathan Bunn and his wife, who have been credited as being Pennington's first Methodist family, in 1774.[22] The gracious hospitality of the Bunn family inspired Allen to write about them in *The Life, Experience, and Gospel Labours of the Rt. Richard Allen*. Richard Allen wrote: "There, [I] laboured in that neighbourhood for some time. I found him [Bunn] and his family to be kind and affectionate, and he and his dear wife were a father and mother of Israel."[23] But even as the new Black AME flock was flourishing and being encouraged by White sympathizers such as the Bunn family, the American Colonization Society was gaining strength in neighboring Princeton.

Nevertheless, Joshua Bunn (one of Jonathan's sons), who owned farmland on both sides of Pennington's Main Street, would eventually become known as what local historian David Blackwell described as "the creator of the

Richard Allen

Founded the African Methodist Episcopal (AME) Church in 1794.

Opened his first AME Church - Mother Bethel – in Philadelphia in 1794.

The Right Reverend Richard Allen, founder of the African Methodist Episcopal Church (AME) in 1794. *Author's collection.*

African neighborhood on South Main Street in Pennington."[24] Land records show that in 1850 Bunn sold some of his property to Black AME trustees Sam Blackwell, Thomas Ten Eyck and George Stout with the stipulation that a church be constructed with a minister of the African Methodist Episcopal (AME) faith. Perhaps this is one of the earliest instances of cooperation between White and Black residents in community building. The descendants of enslaved people and a White founding family understood that they shared not only a particular theological view but also an interest in forming mutually beneficial communities. So began one aspect of Pennington's African American community growth as churches rose to the mission of serving as a spiritual, social and political buffer between the Black and White worlds. Over time, other Black denominations followed. For example, the origins of the Hopewell Black church dates back to 1894, when a group of African American Christian men and women met in their homes on Wednesday and Sunday evenings for prayer and fellowship. Within a year, an increasing number of Black Baptist families were arriving from Virginia. A Virginia-born clergyman was the first pastor, Reverend Thomas E. Johnson (1850–1898), recorded in the 1910 census living in Hopewell Borough. He realized that this congregation needed its own place of worship, since many had been relegated to years of sitting in the balconies at local White churches. By 1897, Black parishioners from Hopewell, Pennington and other nearby towns were holding revival meetings in Stoutsburg, New Jersey. The next year, under the leadership of Reverend Johnson, the group purchased a lot on First Street in Hopewell to build the First Colored Calvary Baptist Church. Not long after, church trustees Silas Terry, Edward Waller and Wilson Walker filed for Articles of Incorporation and the church was renamed Second Calvary

The new Second Calvary Baptist Church in Hopewell, New Jersey. *Courtesy of Hopewell Valley History Project.*

Reverend Hurst and Mrs. Hurst in front of the original Second Calvary Baptist Church, circa 1955. Hurst was the fifth paster of the First Colored Calvary Church of Hopewell, New Jersey, located on First Street in Hopewll Borough. *Author's collection.*

Reverend Lawton James, pastor of Bethel AME Church in beginning, with church ladies' auxiliary members, circa mid-1960s. *Courtesy of Shana Jennings-Williams.*

Reverend Lawton James and members of the Bethel AME Church, circa mid-1960s. *Courtesy of Shana Jennings-Williams.*

Baptist Church, with baptisms performed in the Stony Brook tributary across the street from the church.

By 1903, the church had paid off its mortgage—it was reported as "the only negro Baptist Church in the state free of incumbrance." "Real Fire Will Be Used in Service" read the headline in the special section of the *Trenton Times* newspaper that celebrated the church's "mortgage burning."

And Johnson expanded his community building beyond the church and into politics. In 1908, Johnson and his comrade Daniel Wooding, future second pastor of Second Calvary Baptist Church, organized the Colored Republican Club, linking together African Americans who had been voting the Republican ticket, likely in hopes that the political party of Abraham Lincoln would help to bring a good end to the struggle for equality that defined the previous quarter century.

Reverend Johnson died in 1914, and by 1920, the community that Johnson had helped to unite had grown to about two dozen extended African American families, some of them working laborers on local farms, others employed working in White households and many working for the railroad.

The next generation of Second Calvary Baptist Church leaders was equally ambitious. Pastor of the church during the 1950s Reverend John A. Gaines (1925–2009), who had migrated to the Trenton area from South

Euwanda Jennings (*left*), Helen Driver (*center*) and Agnes Stewart (*right*), members of Bethel AME Church, circa early 1960s. *Courtesy of Dorothy Mason.*

Pittsburgh, Tennessee, led his congregation to erect a new building on the southwest corner of Columbia and Maple Avenues in Hopewell Borough in 1959 when Second Calvary had outgrown its building. Four years later, the sixty-six-year-old Second Calvary Baptist Church building on First Street, officially "abandoned," was demolished in a controlled burn by the Hopewell Fire Department, though its burial ground, located behind the original edifice, remains intact. There Reverend Thomas Johnson and his wife, Amanda, are interred, along with several dozen parishioners who migrated from Danville, Virginia area in the early 1940s. There are more than a dozen unidentified, unmarked graves; one of a three-month-old child, Willie S. Young, who died on December 10, 1899, is said to be the first known burial.

The Black congregation, meanwhile, relocated to the newly erected Second Calvary Baptist Church, anchor of the historically Black residential community of Hopewell Borough. And unity between Second Calvary and other African American churches in the region cemented the Black communities. Gathering together not only for worship services but also for civic meetings, fundraisers, church dinners, bake sales, youth programs, social fellowships, weddings, baby dedications and funerals helped all of the congregations to flourish. In addition, Second Calvary Baptist Church has maintained a long-standing relationship with a number of local White churches, through the ecumenical Hopewell Council of Churches, including Hopewell Presbyterian Church (organized 1857), Calvary Baptist Church (organized 1871), St. Alphonsus Roman Catholic Church (organized 1874) and Hopewell United Methodist Church (founded 1893). From grand cathedral-style buildings to small, simple, tranquil chapels, people sought to honor God with these sacred spaces.

The council, created over fifty years ago by the pastors and monsignors of these five churches, along with a variety of laypeople, has remained vibrant for more than a half century. This group is a testament to what can happen when people of strong faith work together to foster ecumenical relations despite racial or social barriers. Each year, on a schedule that rotates among the constituent churches, the council gathers to worship together for Thanksgiving Eve and Lenten services. The pastors rotate speaking at each church, where worship includes music, devotions and liturgical readings.

Nevertheless, even as Hopewell and the surrounding region has been exalted for historic sites and the final resting place for prominent White founding families, the heritage of the founding African American community, families and institutions has largely remained in the shadows—a forgotten people with a rich, varied and intertwining past that also merits recognition.

2

LIGHT ON HIDDEN HOPEWELL STORIES

A little more than five miles due north of Pennington lies the borough of Hopewell, situated not far from the convergence of Somerset, Hunterdon and Mercer Counties. Prior to the Revolutionary War, the small hamlet—initially called Columbia in homage to Christopher Columbus—was renamed Hopewell Meeting and officially changed to Hopewell after the formation of Hopewell Township in 1798.

The first settlements of Hopewell were from land purchases of Edward Burroughs from Long Island in 1694, Roger Parkes Sr. and Roger Parkes Jr. in 1697 and Jonathan Stout in 1706. In 1776, early landowners enslaved people who usually went by an assigned first name. Once freedom was received, it was not uncommon for formerly enslaved people to take the last name of their enslaver or make up a last name of their own. Some of these early pioneers, revered as among the founding fathers of Hopewell, include James Larison, David Hunt, Abraham Golden, John Hart (signer of the Declaration of Independence), Nathan Hixson, Stephen Blackwell, Ebenezer Stout, Andrew Stout and Spencer Weart.[25] From 1751 to 1766, John Hart owned a half share of the Stony Brook Mills at Glen Moore, and at the time of the Revolutionary War, and probably several years previous, owned a two-thirds share of the gristmills and fulling mills at Rocky Hill, which did a large business; his son-in-law, Colonel John Polhemus, owned the other one-third share.[26]

Thus the Hopewell area, with its burgeoning industries, was poised to play a significant role in the Revolutionary War. A few miles outside of the borough, one of General Washington's pivotal war councils—where he planned the 1778 victorious Battle of Monmouth over the British—was held at the Hunt House, the former Stout farm, located on Provinceline Road. Under this roof, a historical gathering of generals, colonels and other notables conferred about what has been considered one of the most crucial battles of the Revolution. Silvia (Sylvia) Dubois, an enslaved individual who died in 1888 at the age of 120, reminisced in her oral biography *Silvia Dubois: A Biografy of the Slav Who Whipt Her Mistres and Gand Her Fredom*. Her interviewer, Dr. Cornelius Larison, recorded Silvia's memory of Washington at the Hunt House:

> *Why the men of the age of my master looked brave. They were tall and commanding and stout of limb, and graceful and handy; they had good faces, great high foreheads, and large bright eyes and broad mouths with good teeth. They stood up straight and walked with freedom and ease. I tell you, in those old times they were good-looking men—brave looking men, they were all so. General Washington was, and Lafayette was, and my master was, and all the great men that I ever saw were, and they were all good dancers and danced wherever they had a chance. They used to say that General Washington was the most beautiful dancer in America—that he could even beat the Markis de Lafayette.*[27]

By 1783, as White New Jersey dwellers had achieved freedom from English tyranny through the American Revolution, an estimated fourteen thousand African Americans remained in bondage. The economic benefits of enslaving human beings was as deeply woven into our region's economy and culture as it was in the southern states. Fear of slave uprisings remained a constant concern for New Jersey slave owners, too. To allay some of these fears, New Jersey legislators enacted laws to control the movements of the enslaved and to mete out harsh punishments for slave resistance:

> *By the slave law of 1714 any negro, Indian or mulatto slave murdering or attempting the death of any freeman, wilful murdering any slave, committing arson, rape on any free subject, or mutiliation of any free person, is to suffer the penalty of death.*[28]

In 1873, as the Somerset County clerk's office was preparing to move to a new location, Revolutionary War–era documents surfaced that revealed particularly harsh punishment for people of color convicted of crimes.

Left: Last Will and Testament of Silvia Dubois, formerly enslaved woman from the Sourland Mountain, who died at the estimated age of 120. *Courtesy of the Hunterdon County Historical Society.*

Right: Silvia Dubois (*right*) with daughter Elizabeth. *Courtesy of the Hunterdon County Historical Society.*

Burning at the stake was commonly used as the punishment for murder, and these events were publicized through newspaper advertisements. In an 1873 *Somerset Unionist* article on court proceedings, it was reported that Colonel McDonald's enslaved man, Jupiter, pleaded guilty to larceny. As such, Jupiter was sentenced to receive "between the hours of one and three this afternoon, twenty lashes on the bare back, and on Monday next the like manner in Pluckamin."[29] The same fate awaited Caesar, the property of David Henry also of Somerset County, who was found guilty of theft. Caesar was sentenced "to receive 30 stripes on the bare back this day at Hillsborough, between the hours of 12 and 3, and on Monday next 39 stripes at the Cross Roads." Tobie, the "Negro slave" of Margaret Middagh, was found guilty of felony and sentenced to be "hung by the neck until he be dead" on the following Saturday, March 15.[30]

Another report regarding harsh punishments occurred on January 9, 1739, in Somerset County when an enslaved man from Rocky Hill attacked

41

an overseer's wife when ordered to fetch firewood. "He pursued her with an axe. The slave killed the overseer's son and then set fire to the barn burning more than a thousand bushels of grain. He was captured and burned at the stake."[31]

Around 1780, near Hopewell Township, Daniel Hart—the brother to John Hart, who was a signer of the Declaration of Independence—was killed by his enslaved man, Cuffee. In *Hopewell Heritage*, author Alice Blackwell Lewis recounted the story of Cuffee's death, inferring that Cuffee was fully responsible for his own death by describing him as "indolent," "lazy" and of "great strength."

Dennis Culliton is cofounder and executive director of the Connecticut-based Witness Stones Project, whose mission is through research, education and civic engagements to "seek to restore the history and honor the humanity of the enslaved individuals who helped build our communities."[32] In this project, Culliton refers to five themes useful in analyzing stories, books or primary documents that purport to chronicle the African American narrative: dehumanization of the enslaved as property, the overall treatment of the enslaved, a paternalistic attitude of the dominant caste, how the economies of slavery played an essential role and human agency and the resistance of the enslaved to make their own decisions to be in charge of their own bodies.[33]

In Cuffee's story, all of these themes are touched on, from the description of the attack on Hart, the outrage of the White neighbors and the subsequent supposed suicide by Cuffee who was fleeing the pursuing mob: "The neighbors were aroused and set out to find the culprit. While hunting for him toward Hopewell, one of the men spied a rabbit and shot at it. Cuffee, hiding nearby, was so frightened by the shot that, on the pretext of borrowing a halter from a farmer to catch a stray horse, used it to hang himself on a tree along Honey Brook."[34]

A poem, written by Hart's neighbor Joseph Titus, who "liked to write history and express himself in rhyme when so doing,"[35] memorialized the event over two centuries ago:

> *Good people all to me give ear, A doleful story ye shall hear, Of a sad murder that was done, Within the bounds of Hopewell town.*
>
> *One Monday morning, as they say, Hart's wicked negro did him slay, He took a knife to win the prize, And like to put out both his eyes.*
>
> *The savage wretch had heart like steel, And no compassion did he feel; He violent hands on him did lay, And with an ax his master slay.*

While he lay gasping on the ground, His life blood swiftly running down, The doctor's help he then did crave, But all his skill could not him save.

He cried for mercy, as they say, The biggest part of all that day; Before the setting of the sun, His life was gone, his work was done.

We leave the dead into the grave, And follow after the black slave, The innocent blood that he had spilt, Shall bring on him a heavy guilt.

Soon as the murder he had done, Then from all people he did run; He took himself oft' to the wood, And there he thought on little good.

The neighbors then for him did look, And found him down by Honey Brook, Hung with a rope upon a limb, No mortal eye did pity him.

The next day they did then prepare, A fire to burn his body there, They chained it to the self same limb, And there they made an end of him.

All negroes who have life and breath, Take warning of his wretched death, Don't take an ax or use a knife, To destroy your master's life.[36]

Almost a half century later, one of the most disturbing lynchings happened to twelve-year-old enslaved James Guild, who was known as "Little Jim." After Catherine Beakes refused Little Jim's request to borrow her rifle to go hunting, Beakes said she believed that Little Jim retaliated by leaving her pen open so that her livestock escaped. The White lady then ordered the boy to leave her property and threatened to report the incident to Little Jim's master. Fearful of this threat, Jim beat the older woman to death and then confessed to the crime and was hanged. Although the presiding judge had been reluctant to execute a child, the conviction called for his punishment to be the same as an adult. And though the case was appealed and debated, the conviction went unchanged, and on November 28, 1828, Little Jim, who was now a fourteen-year-old boy, was hanged on "a scaffold near where the Reading Academy was later built; An empty field back then, the Reading Academy was later built there and was Flemington's only public school from 1862–1915; the site is now the Bonnell Street entrance of the Reading-Fleming Intermediate School."[37] Sylvia Dubois, the enslaved girl

Extract of a Letter from a Correspondent at Princeton, October 28, 1767.

" The Distemper which has been so prevalent among the Horses in the neighbouring Parts, begins also to rage here, tho' I do not hear that it has yet proved fatal to any; the People are however under some Uneasiness left it should prove as mortal as it has been in many other Parts of this and the adjacent Provinces.

" The Negro advertised in your *Chronicle*, No. 39, to have killed his Master Mr. *Daniel Hart*, at *Hopewell*, was found on Wednesday last. It seems he took a Rope from off one of his Master's Horses the Night after he committed the Murder, by which he was found hanging. His dead Body was burnt the Day after."

"A Negro fellow, Cuff" October 12–19, 1767, *Pennsylvania Chronicle. Princeton Slavery Project, https://slavery.princeton.edu/.*

who had been present at the Hunt House during George Washington's 1778 council meeting, also observed this hanging.[38] Did her master require her to attend, in order to remind her of the consequences of Black misbehavior? Or was she simply among the ghoulish onlookers? We cannot know. In any case, as disturbing as is this account of the execution of a child, the narrative did not end there. As reported by Marfy Goodspeed in "Goodspeed Histories, Little Jim Part Three," Little Jim's body "was carted off in a spring wagon to Runk's Mill, in what is now Idell, where by the light of a lantern, Dr. Coryell, proceeded to cut the little fellow up, just what he expected to find I never found out.[39]

3

WHITE AND BLACK BLACKWELLS GROW THEIR LEGACIES

For more than three centuries, there have been descendants of the Blackwell family in Sourland Mountain and the surrounding area. And the Blackwell surname has been memorialized in many aspects of the region: roads, mills and various businesses bear the Blackwell name. Where did the early Blackwell family members come from, and how did they land in the Sourland Mountain region?

Robert Blackwell, who brought the Blackwell name to the American colonies sometime before 1670, was born in England in 1643 to Thomas and Bridget Blackwell. Soon becoming a successful merchant, Robert Blackwell, a widower, lived on Long Island with his two children, Robert Jr. and Ann. In 1676, Robert appears in the records of New York City, where he married a second time to Mary Manningham. Mary was the stepdaughter of Captain John Manning, who was granted an island off the East River in New Jersey in 1667 by Governor Richard Nicolls, the first English governor of the New York province. When John Manning died around 1685, Mary inherited her stepfather's island, which at that time was called Manning's Island. Thereafter, the island was known as Blackwell's Island. Robert and Mary's ten children were to receive this inheritance that Mary had gained from John Manning, which also included a farm on Long Island. Each of Robert's children with his first wife (Robert Jr. and his sister, Ann) was to receive a gift of not more than £200 pounds. Thus was Robert Blackwell Jr. set adrift from the New York family wealth—free to make his fortune elsewhere.

By 1710, Robert Jr., with his good friend John Titus, had relocated to New Jersey, where each purchased sizable landholdings in Hopewell Township. Robert, then thirty-five years old, cleared his land, established a home and farm and married Elizabeth Combs. By the time he was forty-five, Robert and his wife, Elizabeth, were the parents to seven children—Robert, Francis, Thomas, Jacob, Mary, Ann and Elizabeth—with a long-standing friendship with John Titus that would extend well beyond the land boundaries that adjoined their homesteads. John's daughter Susannah married Robert's son Thomas, thereby cementing the Blackwell/Titus connection for the next generation, which included Amy, John, Jacob, Benjamin, Jerusha and Andrew, Robert's grandchildren. When Thomas passed away, he left a 166-acre estate to be divided among sons Andrew, Jacob and Benjamin.

Thomas and Susannah's son Andrew never married, and for the majority of his life, he was a resident of the small hamlet called Mount Rose. Mount Rose, mainly a crossroads connection between Trenton to the south and Princeton to the north, was part of the Hopewell Tract, which consisted of thirty-one thousand acres formed as early as 1707 when it was "re surveyed for Dr. Daniel Coxe in 1707. Ethnically a mixture of English, Scots, Dutch, and French, most residents of Mount Rose were second or third generation 'Americans' although some were Quakers or Baptists, the majority were Episcopalians and Presbyterians. Such was the context into which the New York Blackwell family sank its roots into Hopewell Township which, by 1700, had enough residents to be granted township status."[40]

On April 23, 1775, news of the Battle of Lexington reached Hopewell while people were still worshiping inside the Old School Baptist Church. After the service, Hopewell resident Joab Houghton positioned himself on a large stone block and loudly challenged his neighbors with these words: "Men of New Jersey, the Redcoats are murdering our Brethren of New England. Who follows me to Boston?" Every man answered "I."[41] Houghton's leadership qualities did not go unnoticed. On October 19, 1776, Houghton was made a captain of the Continental army and on March 15, 1777, a lieutenant colonel. He was also a member of the first New Jersey legislature. Andrew Blackwell, living in Mount Rose less than five miles from where Joab Houghton made his plea, heeded the call to fight against the British for freedom, serving as a private in Captain Joab Houghton's Company, Hunterdon Militia. In the struggle for liberty, he took an active part on the side of his country and continued through life the friend of freedom and equal rights.[42]

Information on Andrew Blackwell's postwar life is cloudy. He owned a large plantation, served as an overseer of the highways in 1781 and may have been a proprietor of the Indian Queen Tavern in Trenton, New Jersey, from the early 1800s until his death in 1818. As described by Harry Podmore for the Trenton Historical Society,

> *The United States Hotel was located on the site of the present Trent Theater on the west side of Warren Street. On this site as early as 1788 stood the Indian Queen Tavern. It was built of stone, two stories high, shed, ice house, etc. were in the rear. Early history of the "Indian Queen Tavern" is still somewhat vague. Several names are mentioned in connection with it, but the records are too confused and indefinite to identify any one of them with the occupancy or early ownership of the property. In the Trenton Federalist, December 3, 1818, the place was again advertised for sale by the executors of Andrew Blackwell.*[43]

During the colonial era, taverns served as venues for amusements such as small circuses or traveling shows because many taverns had large yards to accommodate travelers with their carriages and horses.

> *Apparently the most popular public house for these exhibitions was the "Indian Queen" or "United States Hotel," as it was later called. One of the early shows to be given an exhibition at the tavern was the waxworks of Davenport and Street, in 1802. Three years later the "invisible lady" was an attraction, and later came Cesar Casa, of Europe, with his wonderful electrical machine. For many years the Indian Queen vied in prestige with the "Trenton House" and the "American House," formerly the "Rising Sun Tavern" which were also on North Warren Street. While its historical associations were not as renowned as these other public houses, the "Indian Queen" was, nevertheless, a popular resort for travelers to Trenton.*[44]

While it seems that Andrew Blackwell was managing his extensive plantation in Mount Rose and the Indian Queen Tavern in Trenton some ten miles away, there is little information regarding how this was being accomplished. Was it all being accomplished through enslaved, indentured or free workers or perhaps a combination of all of these? Blackwell's will offers little information. Aside from providing for a "servant man Frost," there was no mention of other enslaved individuals. Blackwell left his substantial wealth to his siblings, nieces and nephews, and his allotment of land was subdivided by his executors and smaller sections of land sold. Over the next two decades, these subdivisions paved the way for expansion of the village of Mount Rose, which grew to include a school, general store, post office, shoemaker, wheelwright, harness marker, blacksmith, tavern and distillery.

The Early Black Blackwells

In the Black and White worlds of community building, there has been a continual ebb and flow in this region. But what do we really know about the Black Blackwells? Where do we begin to piece together a puzzle that has not been examined in over two centuries? How did the descendants of these families, though living in separate communities, continue to intersect over time?

It's interesting how the life of one person responsible can change how history unfolds. Were it not for the manumission of Frost and his eventual purchase of his wife and son, would Pennington have such a dedicated community-builder as Samuel Blackwell? The manumission of Frost—Samuel's father—deeply influenced the trajectory of Hopewell Township's Black community.

It was 1819 when Frost, the first recorded Black Blackwell, appeared before the Inferior Court of Common Pleas with executors Isaac Dunn and Benjamin Blackwell, who enacted the terms of Andrew Blackwell's will, legalizing the document that ensured Frost's freedom:

> *It is hereby made known that on the twelfth day of April in the year of our Lord one thousand and nineteen, we Benjamin Blackwell and Isaac Dunn, executors of Andrew Blackwell late of this Township of Hopewell in the County of Hunterdon have liberated manumitt and set free our Negro man Frost and do discharge him of all service or demand of service to be hereafter made either by us or any person claiming by or under us.*

At first glance, Frost's manumission could have been seen as a magnanimous gesture on Andrew Blackwell's part. And paragraph seven, one sentence long, made an additional concession: "I give to Frost my servant blackman his freedom and one hundred dollars." Thus, by the stroke of a White man's pen, a Black man gained not only his freedom but also a gift of money. But does this freedom and a little cash erase all the years of Frost's existence as one human being owned by another? Until

Daniel Stout witnesses document freeing Frost Blackwell from slavery, April 1819. *Courtesy of the Hunterdon County Historical Society.*

the end of his owner's life, Frost was the "servant blackman," *property* listed along with the gifts Blackwell left to his family so carefully enumerated in his will. What remains unknown is the number of years Frost had to serve Blackwell before Blackwell set him "free." Research has yet to uncover any information about Frost's family or community, such as a bill of sale or the mention of other enslaved individuals Blackwell may have owned or anyone living nearby who could have been Frost's parents, relatives or friends. Blackwell, described by his executor as a "friend of freedom and equality," left one hundred dollars for someone who spent more than a third of his life in bondage. Explicitly outlined in his will, Blackwell bequeathed one hundred *pounds* to each of his living brothers, sisters, nieces and nephews; to Frost he left one hundred *dollars*. The differential between leaving pounds and dollars was significant, as in 1817 the pound sterling, though fluctuating somewhat, could be as much as five times the value of the dollar.[45] In addition, the dollar, unlike the pound, would be subject to the solvency of the local bank on which it was drawn.

If Frost's economic life was precarious, his "freedom" was equally so. In 1786, the estimated year when Frost was born, changes were made in New Jersey's manumission laws:

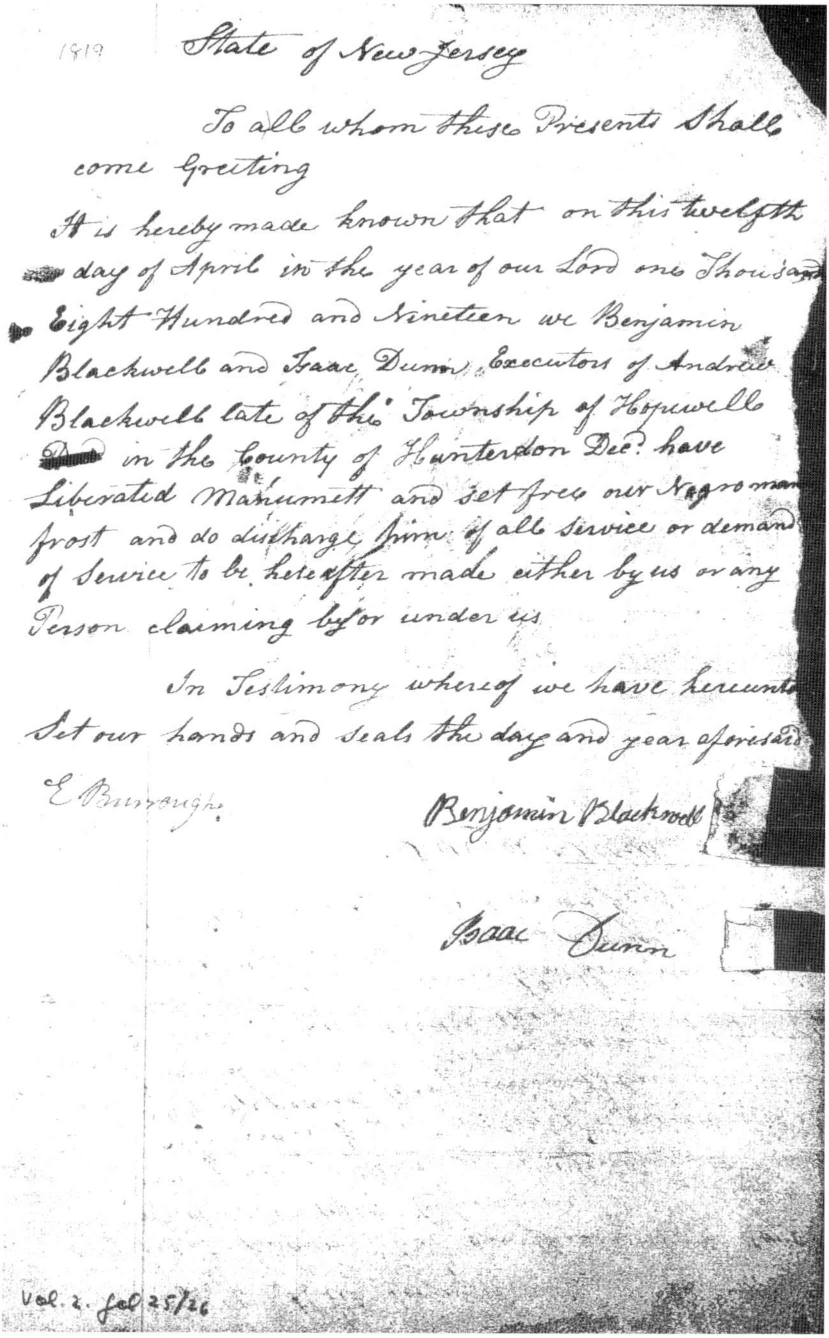

1819

State of New Jersey

To all whom these Presents Shall come Greeting

It is hereby made known that on this twelfth day of April in the year of our Lord one Thousand Eight Hundred and Nineteen we Benjamin Blackwell and Isaac Dunn Executors of Andrew Blackwell late of the Township of Hopewell in the County of Hunterdon Dec? have Liberated Manumitt and set free our Negro man frost and do discharge him of all service or demand of Service to be hereafter made either by us or any Person claiming by for under us

In Testimony whereof we have hereunto Set our hands and seals the day and year aforesaid

E Burroughs

Benjamin Blackwell

Isaac Dunn

Vol. 2. fol 25/26

Frost Blackwell's manumission document, Hunterdon County Inferior Court of Common Pleas, April 1819. *Courtesy of the Hunterdon County Historical Society.*

> *Slaves between the ages of twenty-one and thirty-five, sound in mind, and under no bodily incapacity of obtaining a support, might now be emancipated without security being given for their support. A master must first secure a certificate signed by two overseers of the poor of the township and two Justices of the Peace of the county, showing that the slave met the requirements as to age and health. He might then manumit the slave by executing a certificate under his hand and seal in the presence of two witnesses.*[46]

Eighteen years later, when New Jersey enacted the 1804 Gradual Abolition Act, Frost was estimated to be eighteen years old. However, according to the legislation:

> *Every child born of a slave after the fourth of July of that year was to be free, but should remain the servant of the owner of the mother, as if bound out by overseers of the poor, until the age of twenty-five years, if a male, and twenty-one years, if a female. The owner of the mother must maintain the child for one year; after that period he might, by giving due notice, abandon it. Every negro child thus abandoned, like other poor children, was to be regarded as a pauper of the township or county, and be bound out to service by the overseers of the poor.*[47]

Since Frost was born prior to July 4, 1804, the legislation did not apply to him; he was not eligible for freedom until he was twenty-five years of age. Therefore, freedom depended on the power and choice of his master, Andrew Blackwell.

But the whims of fate worked to Frost's advantage, and on April 12, 1819, Frost appeared in the Hunterdon County Courthouse an enslaved man and left, at the age of thirty-three, an illiterate but free man. When Frost left the courthouse and breathed the spring air, he was officially *Frost Blackwell*—a name he had either chosen or had been assigned, but in either case—a name that would begin a long and fascinating family line.

Census records show that Frost Blackwell remained in Mount Rose. In 1816, two years prior to receiving his freedom, Frost married Nancy Vanvactor, who was still in bondage in Somerset County. Their first son, Samuel, born in 1817, was considered by law to be enslaved because of his mother's status. But Frost had a long-range plan that would change all of this. Perhaps the one hundred dollars Frost received from Andrew Blackwell served as a foundation for Frost to eventually purchase his wife and son. In any case, on April 9, 1827—almost eight years to the day of his own

Stipulation number seven in the Will of Andrew Blackwell granting freedom and one hundred dollars to Frost Blackwell. *Courtesy of the New Jersey State Archives.*

manumission—Frost filed papers to purchase the freedom of his wife, Nancy; apparently, he had saved enough to satisfy her worth. Standing next to Charles W. Stout (who may very well have been Nancy's enslaver), overseers Stephen Titus and James Stevenson and justices Edmund Burroughs and David Stout, Frost attested to the following:

> *Know all men by these present that I, Frost Blackwell of the Township of Hopewell in the County of Hunterdon and State of New Jersey, have liberated, manumitted and set free my female slave, Nancy, at the age of thirty one years or thereabouts I do therefore by these present liberate manumit and set free the said Nancy from all service or demand of service thereafter to be made by me or any other person or persons.*[48]

By purchasing Nancy, Frost ensured his wife's freedom from possible enslavement or threat of sale to anyone else. Thereby, like other free Black Americans, Frost became a "slave owner" as an act of benevolence and self-preservation. As history has recorded free Black people were slave owners "in each of the thirteen original states, and later in every state that countenanced slavery,"[49] Black slave ownership was quite small in comparison to the number of African Americans owned by White people. And an even smaller number of African Americans bought or sold slaves purely as property and/or enforced labor.[50] But Frost was among the majority of free Black slave owners who purchased a family member strictly for the purpose of protection.

While saving to purchase his wife, Frost resided in Mount Rose at the farm known as the Centerville Farm. Owned by Enoch Drake, the property was left in 1822 to one of Drake's sons, William, which stated in the fourth paragraph of his will, "To my son, William, all that farm situate in said Township of Hopewell now occupied by Frost, a free colored man, which

Moore Blackwell (*center*), descendant of Frost Blackwell, along with family members in Princeton, New Jersey. *Courtesy of Shirley Satterfield.*

I value at fifteen hundred dollars."[51] By the 1830 census, it was recorded that a free Black man was living at Centerville Farm with the family of Peter Drake, Enoch's youngest son. Presumably, Frost, as well as his wife and family, were still residing on this farm in Mount Rose.

Frost and Nancy's family grew to include Samuel, Noah, Benjamin and two daughters whose names are unknown. One of the daughters may have been named Harriet. The 1840 census indicates that Frost, a woman, three boys and a girl were all living north of Hopewell. And Frost's children were soon putting down roots nearby. In 1857, Frost's sons Samuel and Noah jointly purchased a nearby house and lot from Andrew B. Drake (a nephew of Andrew Blackwell).[52] Census records indicate that Samuel had been a property owner in Pennington for at least a decade and apparently by 1860 Nancy also was living in Pennington either with Samuel or with Harriet Brister, who may have been her daughter. During that decade, apparently, Frost passed away, as he does not appear in the 1860 census. When Nancy died in 1882, she was mentioned in the September 13, 1882 issue of the *Hopewell Herald*: "Died, Nancy Blackwell, a black woman and the oldest resident of Pennington, aged 88."[53] Thus, Nancy Blackwell—who was born one year after the American victory of the Revolutionary War had "freed" the White Blackwells—gained her freedom through her husband's purchase of her body and had lived long enough to see all Black Americans freed when slavery was prohibited through the Thirteenth Amendment.

4

OLIVER HART AND FRIDAY TRUEHART BRING THEIR LIVES TO HOPEWELL BOROUGH

O n a crisp day on December 2, 1749, the Reverend Oliver Hart stepped off the coastwise vessel *St. Andrew* in Charleston after a nineteen-day trip from Philadelphia; he was heeding the call to pastor the Baptist Church. Hart, a young man of twenty-six, was described as "tall and well-proportioned" and could not have known of the tumultuous times and seasons with which God would match his life in Charleston.[54] From this time forward, Hart would become known as one of the most influential preachers among South Carolina Baptists.

During his thirty-one years of pastoring, Hart was known as not only a respected Baptist leader but also a devout advocate for freedom from British rule. His commitment to secure the liberty of the colonies caused Hart to flee Charleston before the British invasion of the city. On November 5, 1780, he traveled north to visit the Old School Baptist Church in Hopewell, New Jersey, and there he was invited to preach. On this first visit to the Old School Baptist Church, he was inspired to use Romans 1:15 for his text.[55] By his second visit on December 16, he wrote in his diary, "This day the members of Hopewell Church being met sent for me and unanimously gave me a call to serve them until spring which I accepted."[56]

Thus, in 1780, Hart began a calling that would last not just "until Spring" but for many years. Founded in 1712 and originally referred to as "Hopewell Meeting House," the building was constructed in 1748 on what became West Broad Street in Hopewell Borough. In 1755, the first pastor, Reverend Isaac

Eaton, established the Hopewell Baptist Academy, the first Baptist secondary school in America.

New Jersey's enslaved population had grown steadily from 1737, when it was recorded there were 3,901 enslaved individuals, and continually increased to 11,423 by 1790.[57] When Hart arrived that chilly December morning to serve the Baptist Church, he was bringing another person—to *serve* himself—an enslaved thirteen-year-old boy named Friday. The mention of this enslaved boy first appeared in Hart's diary, which has been described as a document that "leaves the impression that Hart was a person of little emotional response."[58] In 1771, nine years before his arrival in Hopewell, Hart wrote in his diary: "Dinah and her son Friday were bought April ye 9th 1771. Dinah was then supposed to be about twenty years of age. Friday was born May ye 29th 1767. The two cost 356 pounds."[59]

IN MEMORY

Of the thousands of enslaved members of the First Baptist Church of Charleston whose names we do not know, but are written in the Lamb's Book of Life.

Revelation 7:9

Hart stayed in Hopewell for the next fifteen years, during which time his slave, Friday, grew to adulthood. By 1791, as his health began to fail, Hart penned his will in a concise and deliberate script, enumerating his wishes item by item. After all debts and funeral expenses were paid, Hart bequeathed his worldly possessions to his second wife, Anne, and his remaining children. Hart left detailed instructions about who would receive the horses, cattle, furniture, china, books, bibles, money and the *human* property as well. Dinah, the "Negro woman" (presumably Friday's mother referred to in his 1771 diary entry), was to become the property of Hart's daughter-in-law Sarah. As the widow of Hart's son, Sarah was instructed to sell "said wench" (Dinah) should she remarry, and the money arising from the sale should be used for the maintenance of her children until the youngest reached the age of eighteen, at which time any remaining principal was to be divided among them.[60] The enslaved man, Friday, along with Hart's watch chain, silver soup spoon and silver pepperbox, was left to Hart's son John.

But before he died, Oliver Hart added a codicil to the 1791 will. In this new will, Hart rescinded the bequest of Friday to son John. Instead, he directed his wife, Anne, "to dispose of Friday's time and labor, or any profits arising there from as she may think proper, after the expiration of seven years." Was this revocation an act of benevolence or more about the protection of the

Charleston Baptist Meetinghouse c1749

Opposite, top: Sketch of Reverend Oliver Hart, pastor of the First Baptist Church in Charleston, South Carolina, and the Old School Baptist Church in Hopewell, New Jersey. *Courtesy of the First Baptist Church of Charleston.*

Opposite, bottom: Present-day plaque in the First Baptist Church of Charleston commemorating the service and memory of Reverend Oliver Hart. *Author's collection.*

Above: Early sketch of the Charleston Baptist Meeting House, circa 1749. *Courtesy of the First Baptist Church of Charleston.*

estate? It is more likely the latter since the 1786 Manumission Law would have put Friday at age twenty-six in 1793 when the codicil was written. At any time prior to this legislation, Hart had the ability to free Friday, but he had chosen not to do so. In 1796, when Hart died, Friday was twenty-nine years old. Adding seven additional years to his "service" would have made him thirty-five, which legally would have indemnified Anne Hart from being responsible for Friday in his "old age."

and before He arrives at the Age of Twenty one Years, my Will is that his Mother shall have the use of said Monies during her natural Life, and at her Death, it shall go to my Children, then living, share and share alike. Or should all these be dead, then it shall go the Philadelphian Baptist Association, to Educate young Men for the Ministry.

Finally. I do hereby nominate, constitute and appoint my beloved Wife Anne Hart Executrix, and my much respected Son-in-Law, Col. Thomas Screven, of South Carolina, together with my esteemed Friends Samuel Stout Esquire and Deacon James Hunt, both of Hopewell, Executrix and Executors of this my last Will and Testament; hereby revoking and disannulling all other Wills, and Testaments, by me, at any Time heretofore made. In Witness whereof I have hereunto set my Hand and Seal. Dated at Hopewell, New Jersey aforesaid, this Sixteenth Day of December, in the Year of our Lord One thousand seven Hundred and ninety one.

Signed sealed and delivered
in the Presence of us.
John Blackwell.
N. V. Randolph
                                        Oliver Hart
Col. H. Black...ll.

A Codicil to the above Will; made and done by me Oliver Hart of Hopewell New Jersey, this fifteenth Day of January one thousand seven hundred and ninety three.

Whereas, by the abovesaid Will I have given and bequeathed my Negro Man Friday to my Son John Hart, I do hereby revoke that Bequest, and my Will now is, that the said Negro Man Friday, shall be fully and absolutely free, at the Expiration of seven Years after my Decease. During which Term of seven years, said Friday shall shall be under the Care and Controul of my dear Wife Anne Hart, to dispose of his Time or Labor, or any Profits arising therefrom, as she may think proper. And in Lieu of Friday, I give and bequeath unto my Son John Hart, Dr. Gill's Exposition of the Bible, in nine Volumes Folio—Body of Divinity, three Volumes Quarto, and on the Canticles, one Volume Quarto, to Him and his Heirs for ever, any Bequest in the above Will notwithstanding. In Witness whereof I have hereunto set my Hand and seal the Day and year above written

In presence of
Benjamin Hixson,
John Blackwell
Edw. Cooper   Oliver Hart

Opposite: Codicil to the 1793 Will of Oliver Hart rescinding his "gift" of Friday and adding additional years of servitude under Hart's wife, Anne. *Courtesy of the New Jersey State Archives*.

Above: Cabin in the Sourland Mountains where Friday Truehart lived with his family after his manumission. *Author's collection*.

One explanation of how Friday received his surname was related by local historian Alice Blackwell Lewis (a descendant of the White Blackwell family) in her recounting of the Hart family's arrival in Hopewell: "Rev. Oliver Hart had a faithful and trustworthy slave. Because of his fondness of this man, he called him Friday True. Later this servant wished to have the name of his master added, so he called himself Friday Truehart."[61] It has yet to be firmly determined whether this name was assigned to him by the court during his manumission. In any case, by 1802 Friday Truehart was able to begin a life where his choices were his own. One such life choice was his marriage to Judah (Juda) Shue from Somerset County. The couple made their home in a log cabin tucked away in the Sourland Mountains, where they raised three sons: Isaac, Aaron and Moses. While little is known about Judah or about whether the couple consciously named their sons to reflect their knowledge of the Bible,[62] Friday and Judah's family apparently thrived.

Fifteen years later, in 1817, Friday Truehart purchased from Andrew Weart and his wife, Rebecca, a 20.57-acre tract of land for $617.10 in Hunterdon County.[63] For the Trueharts and their descendants for the next century and beyond, so began property ownership and deep community roots. Following his father's lead, Isaac Truehart bought, in 1828, three lots of land in Hopewell Township, totaling sixteen acres for the sum of $400.14.[64] Thus, as the heir of the deceased Stephen Blackwell (of the White Blackwells) sold a homestead to Isaac True, "a free coloured man," the continuing connection between the Trueharts and the Blackwells (both Black and White) would be cemented.

5

LOOKING BACKWARD

WHITE BLACKWELLS, BLACK TRUEHARTS

William H. Truehart (1845–1932), the son of Isaac and Martha Truehart and grandson of Friday, grew up on the farm his father had created on the land he'd bought from the estate of Stephen Blackwell. William Truehart's world included a "beautiful garden, and fruit trees and berries that grew in abundance."[65] For the majority of his adult life, William Truehart worked as a servant and coachman for Jonathan Hunt Blackwell and his family in Trenton, New Jersey. Jonathan, one of Stephen Blackwell's sons from Hopewell, married Susan Weart, also from Hopewell. Jonathan and Susan had four children: Clara, William, Henry and Stephen, who died in the sinking of the *Titanic* along with his friend Washington A. Roebling while returning from a European tour.

In June 2019, a descendant of the White Blackwells—then eighty years old at the time—reached out to the Hopewell Museum to share a "memory" that had been written by her mother titled "My Most Unforgettable Character," recounting a story about a person whom her mother considered to have left a lasting impression in her life. Along with this document was an inquiry regarding the possible donation of a custom-made box by this person, which her mother had passed down to the family.

Born in 1908, her mother, Elizabeth, reminisced about growing up in the home of her grandparents Jonathan and Susan Blackwell and that family's five-plus-decade relationship with William "Billy" Truehart. Elizabeth Twyeffort wrote:

When William was about thirty years of age, he came from the country to work for my Blackwell grandparents as coachman in Trenton, New Jersey. My grandfather owned a pair of matched bays of which he was especially proud because of their high spirits, and the speed at which they ran. Since these unusually headstrong horses needed a great deal of exercise, William was required to drive them daily down West State Street, following a trolley car. Probably this obstacle in front of them served as a pace setter, and also acted as a brake if they tried to run away. Every Sunday when my father was a little boy, his family went to Hopewell, New Jersey ten miles away in the country to visit cousins. Because of the breakneck speed at which the horses went, he crouched down on the floor of the carriage scared to death! But when the first automobiles appeared on the roads, the horses were sold and my grandfather brought a Stanley Steamer. William never learned to drive a car, and so he became gardener and chore man for the household.

William Truehart was raised near Hopewell in the Sourland Mountains of New Jersey and somehow became the owner of a small property where he had a chicken farm and fruit trees. The whitewashed shack, in which his nephews lived, was set in a veritable Hansel and Gretel woods. Large dark boulders which marked the end of an ancient glacier were scattered through the trees. It was here that William came on Sundays and holidays. He would leave the house in Trenton dressed neatly in a black cloth suit and high crowned derby and walk to the trolley which took him to Hopewell. There he walked up the Rileyville road past the Hill Billy Tavern, across fields for a few miles, finally reaching his own place.

My parents, my two sisters and I lived with my grandparents. Their Greek Revival stone house, painted yellow, was set back from the main street in the center of a large lawn with horse chestnut trees. Along the street front was a wrought iron fence with a small gate at each end and double gates in the center. The latter was only opened by William on the rare occasions of a family funeral.

In late fall William pushed his wheelbarrow slowly and laboriously up the driveway from the barn with a cumbersome load of sections of boardwalk balanced on it, and laid them end to end to make a dry walk from the street to the house. But when the paths were clear in spring, we grandchildren with our bicycles came to the bane of this hardworking man's life, because we carelessly clipped off the neatly cut edges of the paths. Then we got a scolding. And if he caught us hiding in the bushes we not only reaped his ire but that of my grandfather.

On bitter cold afternoons when everyone was either out or taking a nap, we children would explore the house inside from the drawing room to the third floor via circular back stair, which was like climbing a miniature turret of a small castle. Tiring of the house, we walked down the driveway following the high whitewashed fence to the garage-barn. At one end of this wooden building was a small room where William lived, which had a magnificent view.

The garage was built on a slope between the lawn at the rear of the house and the canal. In between the two was a terraced garden where roses climbed the brown stone wall, with peony bushes, strawberry beds, and clumps of different colored iris. Along the bank was a vegetable garden. Beyond the canal a wide park extended along the Delaware River, with a view of both the upper and lower bridges that crossed to Pennsylvania.

We children would cautiously knock on the door hoping William would let us in and play his violin for us. His little room had windows on two sides, and housed the rubber plant from the small conservatory off the dining room. There was a white iron bedstead covered with an old patchwork quilt, a pot bellied iron stove and a few other pieces of furniture. If William was in a receptive mood he would draw his music stand up to a straight chair, put on his steel rimmed spectacles and place his open music in front of him. With gusto he would proceed to play our favorite piece, "Pop Goes the Weasel," while tapping out the time with his soft black boots on an old piece of carpet. His squeaky bow passed quickly over the strings, and as he played, we waited with baited breath for one flat note that he always hit just before the word "pop" plucked with one finger.

William had a strong constitution, was never sick a day until just before he died, and retained all of his teeth. He could bend from his hips and swinging his arms easily from side to side, weed for long stretches of time. He was of medium height and slight of build. There never seemed to be any indecision as to how he would accomplish his many and varied chores. He never had a minute to waste and was always on time from very early in the morning until his early retirement at night. This fine man was well loved and greatly admired by our relatives and friends. In warm weather after raking the leaves under the trees by the front fence, he would lean on his rake, remove the perspiration from his face and neck with a blue and white bandana handkerchief, and rest for a while. Often people would stop and converse with this intelligent, well mannered man calling him "Billy True" by which many knew him, or "Mr. Truehart."

There were endless tasks not only outside the house, but very important ones to be done inside as well. In the late winter afternoons when we arrived home cold and tired, we would go into the library and stand over the floor register to warm our feet and legs. Just below us we would hear the loud scraping of the shovel on the floor of the coal bin. On going down to the basement, we would find William in a blue-checked apron (which he made on the sewing machine), sitting on a chair in front of the open furnace door, waiting for the small blue flames to catch hold and turn to gold. He sat there reading from the pages of his dearly beloved "Sears & Roebuck" catalogue from which he ordered all of the seeds for the garden and whatever he needed for his farm. He also ordered his clothing. His soft high black boots were especially made at the cobbler. After the fire was well started, he would go into the kitchen and take from a cupboard his own special plates, cup and saucer. He ate an early supper alone at the table, while the cook was preparing dinner. For many years he ate only a bowl of corn meal mush and drank a cup of tea; in his late years he would take only a cup of hot water and a piece of toast. When he was finished eating he washed his dishes and returned them to the cupboard. At breakfast the cook served him dinner from the previous night, including dessert even if it was ice cream.

William's first duty of the day was to tend the furnace. At five thirty every bleak bitter cold morning, if we awoke, we heard outside our windows the scrape of metal ash cans being carried up the stone basement steps to be put on a wheel barrow; then steps on the gravel driveway as William pushed the load out to the front walk. Soon after came the running footsteps of the milk man with the milk bottles rattling against his metal basket. He did not have to hunt for a scribbled note telling him of the day's order, because our ingenious handy man had invented a simple box with a sliding lid. Across the top were the metal letters, P/C, Q/M and P/B. Under each letter was a lid when pulled out ahead of time, revealed large nail heads in a straight line. All that anyone had to do was count them; and that was how the milk man knew what was needed; pints of cream, quarts of milk and pounds of butter.

When we were at the breakfast table, William, all smiles, would go to the head of the table, spread a small cloth on the rug, and place on it his shoe shining stand, and his box of implements. While grandfather, and then later on my father sat there, they would put aside the morning paper to chat and joke with him, while he shined their shoes. If it was very cold weather they would ask him the temperature, and if it was cold enough for the canal to freeze, William would be asked to pass judgment on whether it was safe for us children to skate. We never disobeyed the verdict because of the warning as to the swift current, which was so dangerous.

It was in the 1920s when Mr. Charles Lindbergh was buying property in the Sourland Mountains of New Jersey that he found that William owned the land next to his. He decided to have his real estate agent try to buy it from him. The agent was a friend of my father's, and that was how we learned of the following: Mr. Lindbergh, knowing who William was, walked over to call on him one Sunday and greeted him by saying, "How do you do Mr. Trueheart?" William, who had never seen the blonde stranger, but surmising who he was—and having refused his offer several times—replied with dignity, "I believe that you have the advantage of me, sir." He had not been properly introduced to this well known man, and he never did sell his property to Mr. Lindbergh.

This fine worker was very strong muscled and well coordinated. He could do everything from mowing the lawn, washing the large windows, handling heavy screens, polishing brass fireplace fenders, gardening, snow shoveling, to turning the handle of the ice cream freezer. When spring cleaning time arrived, he rolled up the heavy rugs and spread them out on the back lawn to beat them with a wicker carpet beater. This was hot work, and those rugs must have been very awkward to balance on his shoulders. In summer when we were away at the seashore, the men of the family commuted to the city every day. It was William who cooked lunch for them, and made the rice pudding that was famous in our house because it was said to be so rich and creamy. Nobody else could make it as deliciously as he did. At the end of the day when the train from town pulled into the platform and we swarmed out of the open touring car to greet the men, we would be presented with a shoe box full of sweet peas from William's garden and often string beans and other vegetables.

On holidays it was his job to put a ladder up to the attic ceiling and climb through a trap door to get the flag out of the trunk. He knew which holiday called for the large cotton one, or the smaller beautiful taffeta one. It must have been as the result of opening of the attic and the hall window on the top floor that soon someone would see a bat soaring through the upstairs hall. Then consternation would arise until some hearty soul tweaked it downstairs with a broom, if William couldn't be found to do it. When William had been with us forty years my father surprised him by giving him a special birthday cake with 40 lit candles and forty crisp new one dollar bills.

It was getting more difficult to hire a competent cook and so William's niece, Anna, came to work for our large household. She was a short, stout, elderly woman and was a good cook. But she finally left us to work at a duck farm up the river as she said that she could make more money plucking ducks.

Years went by and progress began to encroach on our city property. Our house and barn were sold to the State of New Jersey about 1930 to build an office building and a parking lot (the location of the barn and William's room). My parents were renovating an old property in Bucks County, Pennsylvania just across the river from Trenton. "Greenwood" had been built in 1804 by George Clymer, a signer of the Declaration of Independence.

William had to move in with his niece who had a little house on an alley not far away. But after a few days, William was so homesick for us all that he begged my father to let him fix a temporary place in our basement for him, until we moved. We had not planned to take William with us, as now he was nearing eighty years of age. It was through cousins that we learned that poor old William was very upset because he thought that we did not want him with us any longer. My father, on hearing how unhappy William was, put him in his car and drove him across the river to the now nearly ready house. Here was a fine room for William. On one side there was a basement room that opened out on a terrace with a well; below this a stream flowed through Japanese iris, down the lawn under pine trees, with a lovely view of fields beyond. After we moved, William walked across the bridge every day to watch the demolition of the old city property.

A few more years went by with the work being handled by a young man, but William still continued to do his gardening. One day he became ill and then had to be taken to the hospital. In a few days he was gone, having lived to be over eighty years of age and having worked for fifty years for four generations of our family. He had been our guardian angel, our friend, a hard working reliable man with ingenuity and intelligence which he brought to every task that he performed. It seemed like the end of an era when he passed away. Everyone who knew "Billy True," or even heard of him such as the younger generations, remembered his fine reputation. He was a truly respected and admired member of our family, and a very important part of our lives. Well named was our "Billy True"—William Truehart.

It was a little more than a century after the Truehart family's purchase of the Sourland land that William Truehart had his unfortunate encounter with Charles Lindbergh in the 1920s. Resisting Lindbergh's proposition to purchase his family's forty-acre homestead, Truehart said, "To some people their native house means everything—more than all the money in the world."[66] As he grew older, William Truehart left his home to live with his niece Martha but made it clear, "I'll never sell as long as I live."[67] William Truehart was good for his word; he never sold even though he never set foot on that property again.

On May 5, 1932, the *Hopewell Herald* reported the death of William Truehart at the age of eighty-seven. He was funeralized in the Old School Baptist Church, the same church in which his grandfather Friday received spiritual nourishment from his enslaver, the Reverend Oliver Hart. A neighbor of the Trenton Blackwell family felt so moved he wrote a poem about William Truehart as a gesture of honoring William Truehart's memory:

William Truehart
Black of skin, and white of soul
Loyal, tried and true.
Faithful servant of this house
Naught too hard to do.
Always working, day or night,
To make things spick-and-span.

A gentleman, inside and out,
Surely an upright man
If faithful service here on earth
Means aught when you depart
Heaven will surely welcome you,
Our William B. True heart.[68]

Top: Suzanne Thompson, Katherine Gaines and Elizabeth Twyeffort, granddaughters of Henry and Katherine Blackwell, who were employers of William Truehart. *Courtesy of Susan Twyeffort.*

Bottom: Greenwood, built in 1804 by George Clymer, a signer of the Declaration of Independence, where the Blackwell family lived after leaving Trenton in the 1930s. *Courtesy of Susan Twyeffort.*

Blackwell House on Blackwell's Island, New York. *Library of Congress.*

Governor Woodrow Wilson
being welcomed to The Inter-State Fair, Trenton, N. J.,
by J. H. Blackwell, President of the Fair

Jonathan Hunt Blackwell greets Governor Woodrow Wilson at the State Fair in Trenton, New Jersey. *Courtesy of Susan Twyeffort.*

Left: Henry C. Blackwell and Katherine, parents of Elizabeth Twyeffort. *Courtesy of Susan Twyeffort.*

Right: A 1938 *Baltimore Afro-American* article on "Old Billy Truehart." *Courtesy of the* Baltimore Afro-American.

6

THE WHITE AND BLACK BLEW FAMILIES

Nancy Blackwell was not the only elderly Black woman to leave her mark on the Hopewell region's race-relations story. Judith, or Juda, Blew, who died in 1857, went from enslavement to freedom through a special arrangement brokered by her former enslavers. Census and taxation records provide a chronology of her life, beginning with a description as "Negro wench" on the 1786 inventory listing of her master, Michael Blew, and including the 1801 Montgomery Township election in which she may have had the distinctive honor of being one of the earliest Black female voters in the history of New Jersey, casting her ballot during the small window before—in 1807—the state legislature restricted voting to White male landowners.

Michael Blew—who descended from the White Blew or "Blau" family—lived in Stoutsburg with his wife and two sons. The Blews were among several Dutch families who migrated to Somerset County from New York in the eighteenth century. The first member of the Blew family to arrive in the region was patriarch John Blew, who owned about 500 acres in today's Blawenburg, a town named after the family. Michael purchased land from his father where he operated his mill. Along with his mill, Michael had a substantial farm of 360 acres that was cared for by enslaved people—two adults and five children—who were listed among his possessions when he died in 1786.

Michael's only "taxable" adult was Tom (valued at £50), who appeared on the inventory list along with "Jonah" (most likely Judith, Tom's wife, who was also called Judah) and child (their baby, son Moses) at £64 or £69, boy Charles (£45), boy Neane (£40), boy Joshua (£30) and girl Patti (£20).[69] Advertisement of Blew's inventory in the newspaper described them as "a likely negro wench, 3 negro boys, and 1 girl from 4 to 14 years old."[70] There has never been information regarding these children, whether they were all the children of Tom and Judith and/or when and how they came into the possession of the Blews.

Michael Blew's death posed a significant problem: remarried at age sixty-five to a much younger woman, he left two sons who were too young to manage the estate. Hence, Michael's wishes could not be fully realized until one of the sons reached legal age. In 1788, two years after Michael's death, it became clear that Michael Blew's records revealed that "Negro Tom," his enslaved Black man, had been liberated by having paid ten pounds to Michael Blew. No longer enslaved, "Negro Tom" was *leasing* 210 acres of the Blew farm in a "sharecropping" agreement. And though the "negro wench"—presumably Judith—was left to his widow, Michael Blew's widow chose not to keep Judith enslaved. The story becomes more complex: apparently, in 1793, when Daniel Blew (the elder of Michael's young sons) reached the age of twenty-one, he took possession of exactly 210 acres—perhaps the same acreage that "Negro Tom" Blew had leased from Michael Blew. The complexities arising from Michael Blew's landholdings and Tom's farm acreage may never been known. In 1793, Daniel Blew's name appeared on the tax list, and Tom Blew's listing of 210 acres disappeared.

But Tom Blew apparently persevered, and his name reappears on the Montgomery Township tax list in 1802, which described him as a "householder" with two horses, two cows and one dog but no indication that he owned any farm acreage—though he may have owned some land in 1801, when it possibly could have been Judith who exercised her right to vote.[71] Tom Blew's landownership is unclear, since at this time of early voting, Thomas would have been eligible to vote as a tenant or land steward since there was no real system in place to register voters strictly based on property *ownership*.

By 1805 Tom had died, and deed records showed that Judith and her son, Moses, purchased a half acre of land from Susannah Lane, a White widow, with whom they may have been employed that same year. After her husband's death, Judith's involvement in the community continued and extended to her joining the Old School Baptist Church in 1809, where she remained an active member for several years.

Signatures from 1801 Montgomery Township, New Jersey poll book with the name of Thomas and what appears to be "Jude" Blew. *Courtesy of the New Jersey State Archives.*

Montgomery Township, New Jersey tax ratable list from 1802 recording Thomas Blew (Negro). *Courtesy of the New Jersey State Archives.*

The story doesn't end there. In 2020, when the Museum of the American Revolution was preparing for an upcoming exhibit titled *When Women Lost the Vote*, researchers examining the 1801 Montgomery County Poll List concluded that Sourland Mountain people of color may have voted in this election—a right to vote under the provisions of New Jersey's first constitution adopted in 1776. It is certain they could not have imagined that their right to vote would soon be rescinded in 1807, when African Americans and White women would be disenfranchised until the passing of the Fifteenth Amendment in 1870 and Nineteenth Amendment in 1920.[72]

In any case, the 1802 story remains blurry. Close examination found that handwritten names recorded by pollsters were ineligible in some cases and an electronic scanning device has raised the question of where it has been thought to be "Jude" may, in fact be "Isaac." Nonetheless, Thomas Blew, Ephriam Hagerman, Henry Lane and Cesar Trent, all Black men, were clearly recorded on the Montgomery County poll list as voters alongside former slave owners, such the Vandevere, Dubois, Duryea, Stockton, Skillman, Stryker and Stout families.

In 2020, the New Jersey Historical Commission, the NJ Historic Trust and the Alice Paul Institute hosted virtual tours to commemorate female voters in New Jersey who voted in those early days and subsequently lost the vote. And although Jude Blew's voting remains in question, the New Jersey Historical Commission paid a tribute to her rise from slavery to landowner.

Signatures from 1801 Montgomery Township, New Jersey poll book. *Courtesy of the New Jersey State Archives.*

Who Was Judith (Juda) Blew,
a Scripted Interpretation[73]

I usually got up long before the family. One of the first things I did before the sun rose was to make sure I got the fire going and start breakfast for the family and the other slaves. Me, my husband, Thomas, the young boys Charles, Neane and Joshua and the girl, Patti, always had a full day of work ahead of us. There was a lot to do on 360 acres of farmland, and we did what we had to inside and outside the house. Sometimes I worked outside right along with the men, but usually I stayed inside and helped the mistress with cooking, cleaning, putting up meat in the smokehouse, making and washing clothes and tending the children. When our mistress died in 1768, Master Michael married a young woman, Nelly, and would have two more children, Michael and Daniel, who I helped her raise.

My master's land is part of 500 acres he bought from his father when the Blew family first came from New York along with other Dutch families. Blawenburg is named after the Blew family and is where Michael Blew operated a mill. When Master died, we didn't know what was going to happen to us Black people because we could all be sold away. The newspaper said the slaves were to be sold separately from the farm equipment and household goods which could mean the younger ones would go together and not be split up. My husband, Tom, was valued at fifty pounds; me and my baby, Moses, were sixty-four or sixty-nine pounds; Charles, forty-five pounds; Neane, forty pounds; Joshua, thirty pounds; and Patti, twenty pounds. Master's will described me as a "negro wench" and left me to Nelly, my mistress. I don't know why my mistress did not keep me as a slave, maybe because she needed Tom to run the farm until her young ones were old enough to take over. So two years after the master's death, the estate paid ten pounds for Tom to be freed. Tom was given his freedom and an arrangement was made for him to lease 210 acres out of 360 acres, and the profits would be divided between the White Blew family and us, the Black Blews.

By 1788, me and Tom were both free and worked the land for the next five years until 1793, when the oldest son, Daniel, took possession of the 210 acres we farmed. After that, Tom no longer appeared on the tax list but was back on nine years later.

But here is the remarkable thing that happened in Rocky Hill in Montgomery Township, Somerset County, New Jersey in October in 1801—Tom and I both voted. On the list I was the only African American female along with three African American men to vote in this election. But Tom and I were the only African American couple who were married who voted. I have been referred to as a "negro wench," and tax records would have you to believe my name was Juda. But my name was Judith, and I went from slavery to freedom and I voted—yes, I voted!

I was laid to rest in 1857 in the ninety-fourth year of my life. And although I was a long-standing member of the Old School Baptist Church in Hopewell, New Jersey, I was buried in the Stoutsburg Cemetery in Hopewell Township on Provinceline Road, where Black people went to be buried. We wanted a burial ground that was not segregated like in other cemeteries, where the Black people were placed away from White people. My son Moses was one of three Black men who purchased that land that is now Stoutsburg Cemetery. I'm not sure if my husband is with me, though I believe he is. I have a headstone that still stands to this day.

In the years to come, if somebody should come along to try to tell my story they will find little to no information about my life. Like most African Americans of my time, records about me were not kept. I have been called Judith, Jonah or Jude or "negro wench." I just hope that one day someone will be able to weave enough strands of my story together so that history will not forget me, especially surrounding the mystery of my name and the 1801 vote in Montgomery Township.

7

LOOKING BACKWARD

EDWIN OLEN "TED" BLEW

ON LEARNING THE NAMES OF MY ANCESTOR'S SLAVES

On January 16, 2022, Edwin "Ted" Blew recorded his continuing sorrow and conflict over part of his heritage.

On a beautiful slope in the foothills of the Sourland Mountains, above present-day Blawenburg, New Jersey, a place near Princeton named for my Blaw/Blew ancestors, lies an eighteenth-century cemetery for African American slaves called the Stoutsburg Cemetery. In the summer of 2018, I stood there, at the gravestones of an African American Blew family, and it was there and then that my eyes were literally opened, for the first time, to the details of the connection between my family and the African American Blews of that area.

The inventory of my fifth great-grandfather Michael Blew's [1704–1786] estate contains the following entries showing the values assigned to each enslaved person:

Negro Man named Tom—50 English pounds
Negro Woman named Jonah and Child—65 English pounds
Negro Boy named Charles—45 English pounds
Negro Boy named Neane—40 English pounds
Negro Boy named Joshua—30 English pounds
Negro Girl named Patti—20 English pounds

Jonah [called "Judah" or "Judith"] was Tom's wife, and their child's name was Moses. Judith died in 1857 in her ninety-fourth year, and Moses, born about 1787, died in 1874 at age eighty-eight. Tom died by 1805, much earlier than his wife and son.

Michael Blew, a mill owner and descendant of Dutch colonists who settled in New Amsterdam in 1652 and migrated to the western district of Somerset County, New Jersey, before the American Revolution, perpetuated the Dutch practice of slavery until his death in 1786, when his estate paid for "liberating Negro Tom," almost eighty years before New Jersey abolished slavery completely, the last northern state to do so.

On that day in 2018, as I gazed at the gravestones of Judith and Moses Blew, I and other attendees of a reunion of the white Blew family listened carefully as Elaine and John Buck and Beverly Mills, compilers of local African American histories, told of the enslavement of members of this Black Blew family by our ancestor. As an active family historian, I remember feeling very excited then at learning about these previously unknown details of our family history. That excitement was quickly tempered by a profound shame and sadness at the realization that my Blew ancestor enslaved and exploited these people.

In the valley below the Stoutsburg Cemetery, just a mile or so away, lies the Blew Family Burial Grounds and the grave of Michael Blew. I've stood in front of his crude gravestone many times and (with the benefit of a more enlightened perspective) asked him the hard questions he may have asked himself: Why did you perpetuate the practice of slavery? Did you know slavery was wrong? Did you ever consider freeing your slaves? If so, why didn't you? Could your milling business have succeeded just as well if Tom had worked together with you as a free person?

The knowledge of ancestral slaveholding is a hard reality, and it puts an indelible stain on a family tree. At the end of a broken line from my family tree, I made a new family tree for Tom, Judith, Moses, Charles, Neane, Joshua and Patti. It stands as a reminder that these were real people with real names who, because of the inexorable forces of history and unconscionable practices of the privileged, became part of the story of the larger Blew family.

As descendants of slave owners, we stand in graveyards, searching for answers and wishing things had been different. But, in the end, what we must do is shine a light on the past and hope its reflection will illuminate a better path forward for all. We can take some comfort in knowing we're not alone:

> *The Legislature of the State of New Jersey expresses its profound regret for the State's role in slavery and apologizes for the wrongs inflicted by slavery and its after effects in the United States of America; expresses its deepest sympathies and solemn regrets to those who were enslaved and the descendants of those slaves, who were deprived of life, human dignity, and the constitutional protections accorded all citizens of the United States; and we encourage all citizens to remember and teach their children about the history of slavery, Jim Crow laws, and modern day slavery, to ensure that these tragedies will neither be forgotten nor repeated.*
> —State of New Jersey, 212th Legislature, Assembly Concurrent Resolution No. 270, November 8, 2007

In January 2021, Ted Blew talked more about his life experience, the feelings he has about his own life of privilege, about the very mixed heritage his forebears left him and about his desire that America can "build back better":

I was born in 1952 in Bloomsburg, Columbia County, Pennsylvania and grew up in a very small town near there…[an] area, comprised mostly of small farms, [which] lies about halfway between Scranton/Wilkes-Barre in the east and State College at the center of the state. It is bounded on the south by Pennsylvania's anthracite coal mining region where my branch of the Blew family settled in 1796, after leaving Somerset County, New Jersey, where my father was born in 1909.

[When] I left my hometown when I was eighteen, to attend college near Philadelphia, I took with me a set of small-town values, many of which helped me weather some stressful times over the years, and some that I abandoned in favor of more broad-minded views of the bigger world.

I am now retired and live with my wife near New Hope, Pennsylvania, a short thirty-minute drive from Blawenburg, New Jersey, where my Blaw ancestors settled in the early 1700s. For most of my career, I worked in Princeton, New Jersey, and I lived near Blawenburg for several years, often driving very close to my ancestors' homesteads and burial grounds, never realizing my connection to those places. In 2002, when I attended a reunion in Blawenburg, organized by the National Blue Family Association, I was able to trace my lineage to the Blaws who first settled there. Since then, I've visited the Blawenburg and Stoutsburg burial grounds many times. I always feel the conflict between wanting to connect to Michael Blew—my fifth great-grandfather— and wanting to disconnect from Michael Blew the enslaver. At Stoutsburg, I apologize to Judith and Moses Blew, for the sins of my family.

8

PENNINGTON'S BLACK COMMUNITY
SINKS DEEPER ROOTS

S amuel Blackwell and his brother Noah were vitally important in the growth of Pennington's African American community—a community partially anchored by the growth of Bethel AME Church. On January 24, 1837, Samuel Blackwell was married to Maximilla Light by the Reverend John Rue of the Pennington Presbyterian Church. Samuel and Maximilla had ten children: Josephine, Nancy, Sabrina, John, James, Benjamin, Moore, George, Dayton and Samuel Jr. Maximilla and her parents, Delilah and Levi Light, were among thirty-six free Black families living in Hopewell Township and had been members of the Presbyterian Church since 1801. In 1858, when Delilah died, she was commended by clergy as being the "servant until death of Mrs. Solomon Titus." Delilah, or "Dill" as she was called, was also described as the "faithful protector of Susannah Titus."[74]

A story by William Holcombe Titus, the great-grandson of Solomon and Susannah Titus, published in 1973 in Alice Blackwell Lewis's *Hopewell Valley Heritage*, included a favorite memory of Dill. Speaking of Dill Titus, her great-grandson said: "I can see her now in her linen homespun gown. She used to stand silhouetted between me and in front of the fire, looking for all the world like a bolster with a string tied in the middle, and then her grey short hair, and such a black face."[75]

Through the middle decades of the nineteenth century, Pennington's African American families built their homes and sank their roots even more deeply into the land for which their ancestors had paid so dearly. Noah Blackwell, the second son of Frost and Nancy, married a woman named Letta and located his new family on South Main Street, near his brother Samuel. Purchasing from Dr. James B. McNair a spacious lot with 100 feet of frontage (146 feet deep) along South Main Street, Samuel and Maximilla built their home next to the AME Church leader Thomas Ten Eyck. The Black community was further dug in when, on March 8, 1850, Samuel Blackwell, Thomas Ten Eycke and George Stout (each of whom bore surnames that mirrored the names of founding White families still living in the surrounding region) purchased sixty acres of land from Joshua Bunn with the agreement that the land was to be used for the expressed purpose of erecting an African Methodist Episcopal Church. David Blackwell, local historian wrote:

> *Samuel Blackwell acted at several times as an intermediary with Joshua Bunn[, and] Bunn sold six lots between Blackwell and the church, from north to south from 1852 to 1856. The last two lots were sold to Blackwell in 1859 and 1861, and he sold both to Joseph Watson in the next few years. "Following the construction of the church, additional lots of land between Samuel Blackwell's property and the church were sold one by one until eight lots north of the church were purchased and houses built." Samuel Blackwell's 100' frontage was the largest in the neighborhood. In 1860 Samuel is shown in the census as a farmer with $1,600 of real estate, which probably represents two houses on South Main Street. He would have rented nearby acreage to farm. The 1875 map of Pennington shows two adjacent houses owned by him, quite possibly the same property.*[76]

An 1875 Everts & Stewart map outlined the town with Delaware Avenue, one of the primary streets, cutting horizontally across the Main Street. Early illumination for the borough streets was meticulously carried out each evening by Charles Hendrickson, a free-born African American known as "Heavy Dick," who became Pennington's first lamplighter. Never missing a day regardless of the weather, Heavy Dick made his way through town with a specially designed three-wheel cart, where he cleaned and lit each gas lamp. Up and down the streets of Main and Delaware, he would service the lamps, including those in front of homes with the addition of "col" after the surname—homes that belonged to J. Watson, E. Mason, H. Brister, H. Welling, S. Blackwell, T. Ten Eycke and S. Allen, which all had the "col" designation on the map. The assumption was that without this designation,

JOSHUA BUNN & WIFE   )   THIS INDENTURE MADE THIS EIGHTH

                TO   )   DAY OF MARCH IN THE YEAR OF OUR

SAMUEL BLACKWELL   )   LORD ONE THOUSAND EIGHT HUNDRED

THOMAS TEN EYKE   )   AND FIFTY BETWEEN JOSHUA BUNN AND

& GEORGE STOUT - TRUSTEES   )   FANNY HIS WIFE OF THE ONE PART AND

                                    SAMUEL BLACKWELL THOMAS TEN EYKE

AND GEORGE STOUT OF THE OTHER PART TRUSTEES IN TRUST FOR THE USES
AND PURPOSES THEREIN MENTIONED ALL OF PENNINGTON COUNTY OF MERCER
AND STATE OF NEW JERSEY AFORESAID OF THE WITNESSETH THAT THE SAID
JOSHUA BUNN AND FANNY HIS WIFE FOR AND IN CONSIDERATION OF THE SUM
OF SEVENTY FIVE DOLLARS IN HAND PAID AT AND UPON THE SEALING AND
DELIVERY OF THESE PRESENTS THE RECEIPT WHEREOF IS HEREBY ACKNOWL-
EDGED OR HAVE GIVEN GRANTED BARGAINED SOLD RELEASED CONFIRMED AND
CONVEYED AND BY THESE PRESENTS DOTH GIVE GRANT BARGAIN SELL RELEASE
CONFIRM AND CONVEY UNTO THEM THE SAID SAMUEL BLACKWELL THOMAS TEN
EYKE AND GEORGE STOUT AND THEIR SUCCESSORS TRUSTEES IN TRUST FOR
THE USES AND PURPOSES HEREINAFTER MENTIONED AND DECLARE ALL THE
ESTATE RIGHT TITLE INTEREST PROPERTY CLAIM AND DEMAND WHATSOEVER
EITHER IN LAW OR EQUITY WHICH HE THE SAID JOSHUA BUNN AND FANNY
HIS WIFE HATH IN TO OR UPON ALL AND SINGULAR A CERTAIN LOT OF LAND
SITUATE LYING AND BEING IN THE VILLAGE OF PENNINGTON MERCER COUNTY
AND STATE OF NEW JERSEY BOUNDED AS FOLLOWS BEGINNING AT A CORNER
WITH HETTY REASONERS LOT THENCE WEST ONE HUNDRED AND FORTY FIVE
FEET THENCE NORTH THIRTY ONE FEET THENCE EAST ONE HUNDRED AND FORTY
FIVE FEET THENCE SOUTH THIRTY ONE FEET TO THE PLACE OF BEGINNING
TOGETHER WITH ALL AND SINGULAR THE HOUSES WOODS WATERS WAYS
PRIVILEGES AND APPURTENANCES THERETO BELONGING OR IN ANYWISE PER-
TAINING TO HAVE AND TO HOLD ALL AND SINGULAR THE BEFORE MENTIONED
AND DESCRIBED LOT SITUATE LYING AND BEING AS AFORESAID TOGETHER
WITH ALL AND SINGULAR THE HOUSES WOODS WATERS WAYS AND PRIVILEGES

Above: Copy of deed from Joshua Bunn and wife to Trustees of Bethel AME Church in Pennington. *Mercer County, New Jersey Clerk's Office.*

Opposite: An 1875 map of Pennington. *Courtesy of the Hopewell Valley Historical Society.*

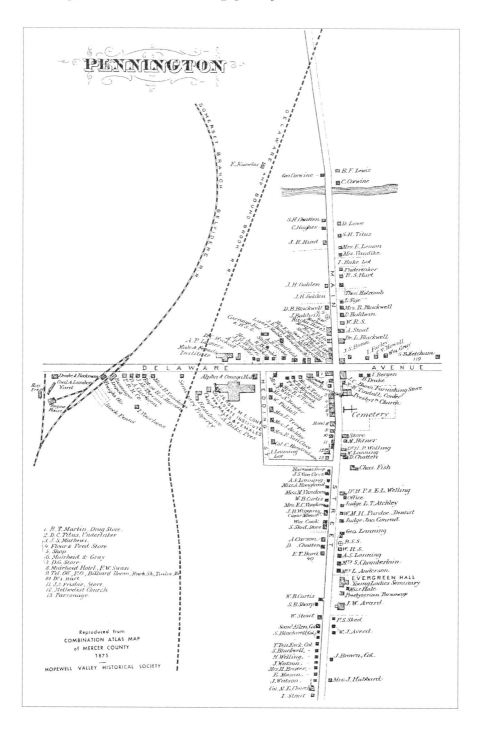

the resident was White. This list also included two additional African American homes—J. Hubbard and J. Brown—on the western side of Main Street on the opposite side of the street from the other "col" homes.

On the same side of the street, north of the row of homes occupied by African Americans, the Evert & Stewart map indicated the homes of White residents: the Welling, Lanning, Fish, Atchley, Stout, Titus, Hart, Holcombe and Blackwell families, which did not have the designation of "col." Though the proximity might suggest a "mixed-race" neighborhood, the Black community, in fact, was clustered at the bottom of a T-shaped borough layout. The appearance of a "racially mixed" neighborhood was also complicated by the fact that the local community had become a welcoming place for some free Black families arriving from the South—some of them with pale skin that could allow them to "pass" for White. This describes such families as the Driver, Caffee and King families, who eventually had made their way to Pennington from Virginia. Through the last decades of the nineteenth century, others came north—also from Virginia—to join family members who had preceded them. Edward Mason, for example, came to join his wife, Sarah, who by 1861 was already living in Pennington on South Main Street in the homestead the family would occupy for thirty-five years before Sarah passed it to her daughter, Rosanna Melinda, in an 1896 will. Rosanna remained in the home for the next fourteen years. Joseph W. Smith took ownership in 1911, and as of this writing, a Smith family descendant remains in the home.

From that Main Street center, the African American community continued to plant free and secure roots in Pennington as their Black brethren were still being held in bondage in the southern states and subjected to the pressures of the 1850 Fugitive Slaw Law that required federal judges and state officials—as well as private citizens—to assist with the mandate to "issue warrants to sale owners, slave catchers, or U.S. marshals to arrest suspected fugitive slaves." The Fugitive Slave Law also stated that "any person who interfered with an arrest, attempted a rescue, or aided or hid a fugitive slave was liable for a $1,000 fine and up to six months in jail."[77] As risky as this was to those who defied the Fugitive Slave Act, New Jersey remained one of the main routes along the Underground Railroad to deliver the enslaved farther north to freedom. But whether the firmly planted Black community of Pennington bravely had a hand in helping those start a new life is a story waiting to be told.

PART II

—◈—

POST CIVIL WAR, THE TWENTIETH CENTURY: BLACK AND WHITE COMMUNITIES OF HOPEWELL AND PENNINGTON CONTINUE TO BUILD

9

TWO BLOCKS AWAY,
BUT WORLDS APART

She was her grandmother's namesake. Nancy, the oldest daughter of Samuel and Maximilla Blackwell, married Joseph W. Smith Sr. in 1872, thus beginning a line of Black Blackwell and Smith descendants that extended into the next century and beyond. According to census records, a male descendant of this Smith family has resided in the region since 1822, beginning with Joseph B. Smith and continuing the lineage with Joseph W. Smith Sr. in 1840, Joseph W. Smith Jr. in 1876, Alphonso P. Smith in 1898 and William W. Smith in 1923. Though records of the Smith line prior to 1822 have yet to be discovered, more than twelve decades of Smith men, and their merger with the Black Blackwells, are woven tightly into the fabric of Pennington's Black and White communities, putting down roots in a mostly all White town. Land development and business opportunities—as well as a fresh start—were available for the enterprising Black immigrants arriving from the post–Civil War south. And the opportunities were expanded by the possibilities of connecting to White entrepreneurs such as William Patton Howe, one of Pennington's most successful businessmen.

Born in 1875 in Hopkinsville, Kentucky, William Patton Howe was raised in Nashville, Tennessee, where his father owned one of the largest ice manufacturing and cold storage companies in the South. In 1909, Howe moved to East Orange, New Jersey, from Kentucky, hoping that a cooler climate would bring relief from the lingering effects of malaria, which he had contracted in South Africa. The following year, Howe migrated

Left: William Patton Howe. *Courtesy of Mary Ellen Devlin.*

Below: Fish Farm, circa early 1900s, purchased by William P. Howe in 1910, renovated to become Dixie Farm. *Courtesy of Elizabeth Berkowitz.*

to Pennington, where he purchased two large farms: one for his family and one for real estate development, which eventually became the Howe-Carroll Company.

After painstakingly transforming the dilapidated family farmhouse into a Georgian Revival–style mansion festooned with a portico and columns, he named his new homestead Dixie Farm—perhaps reflecting his southern upbringing. The splendor of the stately mansion stood in stark and commanding contrast to the borough's more modest Victorian-, Federal- and Four Square–style homes along Main Street. Within a few years, Howe had purchased additional land in the southwest end of town and opened it up for development. This acquisition eventually encompassed more than four miles of new streets with 2,500 newly planted shade trees, which Howe believed would make sidewalks more appealing. Then sidelining his real estate business, Howe opened a wholesale nursery, selling flowers—peonics and iris—to local vendors. Howe's daughter Edna remembered this aspect of her father's life:

> *He and Mother used to like to drive out into the nursery in the evening. Often all of us would go and get an ice cream cone somewhere and drive through the nursery. At one time he was raising nothing but peonies, those great big beautiful pink and white flowers, and there were just acres and acres of them. But he would drive Mother out to the nursery at the end of a long day, and stop and cut off with his penknife that he always carried, a branch of some beautiful piece of flowering shrub and give it to her. We had a very close family life.*[78]

During World War I, Howe converted numerous acres for food production. But by the end of the war, he was again concentrating on developing and expanding Howe Nurseries. In the 1930s, Howe's decision to have the nursery sell directly to consumers opened employment opportunities for townspeople, and this innovative retail market was so successful that he opened other outlets around New Jersey and metropolitan New York. As one of the largest employers in the region, Howe drew heavily on a pool of migrants from Puerto Rico; by 1955, an estimated one thousand Puerto Rican workers had relocated to Trenton,[79] less than ten miles away from Howe Nurseries.

> *The increased migration led to job opportunities at a time when unskilled and semi-skilled labor was in demand and workers' aspiration levels had*

The First Baptist Church
CRAWLEY AVE. AND ACADEMY ST.
PENNINGTON, NEW JERSEY
FOUNDED 1902

To The Howe Family-
We deeply regret the passing of our
friend, Mr. Wm. P. Howe Sr.
We offer our sincere sympathy and
Condolence to the members and friends
of his family.
We thought of him as an understanding
kind, considerate and warm hearted
friend. One always willing to come to
the aid of those in need
Truly we can say he is gone but not
forgotten. His memory will ever linger
in the hearts of all that knew him.
Sadly submitted by the members
and associates of The First Baptist Church.
H. Lewis Minister
Louella Richardson Secty.

Sympathy note from the First Baptist Church of Pennington on the passing of William P. Howe. *Courtesy of Mary Ellen Devlin.*

been raised by schools, radio, newspapers and magazines, and the example of relatives, friends, and neighbors who had previously migrated and had advanced themselves economically.[80]

In addition, Pennington's local African Americans were among those who took advantage of this industry.

Howe, thereby, became well-known among the local Black community. When he died in 1964, the First Baptist Church of Pennington, which was one of the oldest African American churches in Pennington Borough, sent a personal condolence letter to his family:

To the Howe Family, We deeply regret the passing of our friend. Mr. Wm. P. Howe, Sr. We offer our sincere sympathy and condolences to the members and friends of his family. We thought of him as an understanding, kind, considerate and warm hearted friend. One always willing to come to the aid of those in need. Truly we can say he is gone but not forgotten. His memory will ever linger in the hearts of all that knew him. Sadly submitted by the members and associates of the First Baptist Church.[81]

One of these local men whose livelihood came from his connection to Howe was Pennington resident Alfonso Smith, who moved his family to a home on South Main Street that had previously been occupied by the family of Samuel Blackwell Jr.—a home situated a few blocks from William P. Howe.

10

HIERARCHY AND DECENCY

ALFONSO PHILLIP SMITH, GRANDSON OF SAMUEL BLACKWELL

CLARA BELLE SMITH, WIFE OF ALFONSO, DAUGHTER OF BALLARD AND PINKY CLARK

Much of the groundwork underpinning the Black community can be attributed to the foresight and tenacity of Alfonso Smith's maternal great-grandfather, Samuel Blackwell. Of Samuel's ten children, his daughter Nancy was Alfonso's grandmother, having married Joseph W. Smith Sr. Nancy Blackwell Smith also had the honor of being named after her grandmother Nancy Blackwell, Frost's wife.

Alfonso Phillip Smith, often called Fonsie, was the oldest son of Joseph W. Smith Jr. and Cora Houston. Alfonso, a diminutive man with light tan coloring and grayish eyes, was born in Neshanic Station, New Jersey, two decades after Reconstruction. He was the perfect blend of New Jersey's racial story: the son of Joe, whose skin matched the color of steeped black coffee, and Cora, whose light buttercream coloring attested to America's racial blending. Some people may have described Alfonso as snobbish, but he had dreams and aspirations for himself and for his race. He was an example of people who struggled to make their lives as comfortable as possible for their families, even if it required some personal discomfort. So it was with Alfonso, who was dedicated to a hierarchy and held clear ideas about the distinction between what he considered to be "decent colored people" and those he viewed as not. For example, "decent" people kept pristine homes, paid attention to being well groomed and well dressed and eschewed using foul language or drinking alcohol.

By 1911, thirteen-year-old Fonsie had become one of Howe Nurseries most loyal employees, and he would dedicate the next sixty years of his life to the Howe family's nursery enterprise—first to William P. Howe Sr. and then to his son, William P. Jr., known as Bill, before retiring from the Howe Nursery as it was run by its third-generation owner, William P. Howe III, known as Pat. Having begun as a young laborer, Fonsie had been promoted supervisor of greenhouses by the time he retired. Fonsie had started out working in the fields of flowers and shrubs alongside a workforce of Black and Brown men who lived in Trenton along with local White boys with summer or after-school jobs. Many of these men hailed from various southern states or from Puerto Rico; all shared the aspiration of employment and a better way of life for their families. Fonsie, who took his supervisory responsibilities seriously, felt committed to modeling high standards both at work and home—standards, routines and disciplines that he believed Black newcomers should adopt in order to be competitive and respected in the White world. Somewhere— perhaps from his parents—Fonsie had developed standards of what defined "decent" Black people. And so he organized his life within the confines of his idea of decent—perhaps to show White America that he was worthy of inclusion in their communities and/or to be an example to his Black colleagues of what they might aspire to. Fonsie might be described as a snob or as a Black man who used his pale coloring to lord it over his browner brothers. But maybe Fonsie just enjoyed taking pride in his work and his life and relished the fact his resources allowed him to be "dapper."

Whatever his ideas or motivations, Fonsie lived a disciplined and regularized life. Fridays, for example, were special for him, not only because it was payday but also because of his favorite routines and meals. After work, he would bathe, shave and change to a fresh shirt. (His shirts, sheets and pillowcases were delivered weekly from Blakely Laundry, and his wife, Clara, would have placed the crisply starched items in his closet.) Along with his fresh shirt, Fonsie would choose a sports jacket and tie to complement the jacket and then began his half-mile drive north to the bank in his impeccably clean Chevrolet, a make of car he drove his entire life. Fonsie would never consider driving a Cadillac, a car he considered flashy and the choice of lower-class Black people who believed they had "arrived." His attire, he believed, readied him to meet and converse with the townsfolk, who were mostly White. His banking completed, Fonsie would return home to await his dinner of fresh scallops, a luxury many—Black or White—could not afford. In spite of being known for his frugality, Fonsie usually treated himself to this seafood delicacy on Fridays—a delicacy his wife invariably overcooked.

Fastidious appearance and orderliness were Alfonso's evidence of what he viewed as Black "decency." He was not willing to spend his time away from work dressed like he was "nothing." He also extended the discipline and elegance of the horticulture business to his home, where he planted two rows of carefully groomed rose beds that provided a sea of red, yellow and pink blossoms. And in his house a curse word was never to be heard, nor a drop of liquor to be drunk. Clara, the second daughter of Ballard and Pinky Clark, migrants from Virginia, was the glue that kept Fonsie's life in order. Married in 1923, Clara and Fonsie had four children in five years—Evelyn, William, Edythe and Gloria the youngest—and only one grandchild who inherited grandmother Cora's fair skin.

The neighborhood had a number of residents who had loyalty and high hopes for their children and their community. Fonsie and Clara lived next to Howard and Sally Hoagland, who shared their pursuit of decency and order, as they raised five children: Rosalie, William, Ellen, Calvin and Chester, who they called "Nin." Sally, who had ideas of decency similar to Fonsie's, insisted on meticulous self-presentation and pristine manners. Sally was one of several Black people from the community who had links to a local White employer. And Sally worked under a significant handicap: she had lost the lower half of her left arm while working at the Pennington Prep School, while operating a washing machine that had been nicknamed "The Mangler" because it was known to be dangerous. Since school records do not record the incident, it is unclear whether this traumatic event occurred prior to Sally's marriage or when she was a young mother. Nor is there any record of whether the Pennington Prep School offered any economic compensation for Sally's loss. What is clear, however, is that Sally did not let her disability limit her life. If anything, being released from her job may have emboldened Sally to fully immerse herself in service to her church and to be a model of virtue for her community—and to become one of Pennington's most beloved and well-known residents.

Thus, Fonsie and his neighbors constructed their routines and their civic allegiances. Fonsie's loyalty was to the Howe Nurseries; Clara's commitment was to the First Baptist Church, where she served as the church organist. What she lacked in skill she supplemented with gusto. But, like Fonsie, Clara enjoyed discipline and order. She planned her days so that she could always

Howard and Sally Hoagland, long-standing Pennington, New Jersey residents. *Author's collection.*

be home at noon in order to have a freshly made sandwich—usually ham and cheese on wheat with a sweet pickle relish and mayonnaise spread—placed on the kitchen counter when her husband walked through the back door for lunch. (The sandwich was not to be prepared and placed in the refrigerator to await his arrival. Fonsie and Clara agreed a *freshly made* sandwich and Clara's presence were the essentials of lunchtime.) To avoid dragging dirt into his home, Fonsie would carefully flatten the hem of his work pants and brush any remnants of soil from his trousers. Only then would he enter the house and position himself on a stool alongside the counter to eat his sandwich, which was usually accompanied by either a glass of Tang or iced tea sweetened with extra sugar.

Clara's social life revolved around her family, her Sunday church service and her participation in a card club, which she would periodically host. Members of the card club were the Black ladies from the neighborhood or from nearby towns. The menu would be meticulously planned, leaving nothing to the last minute. Table linens, freshly starched and delivered by Blakely Laundry, arrived along with the bed linens and Fonsie's dress shirts. The tablescape, as important as the lunch that would be served, included roses from the carefully tended flower beds. Clara would take her cutting

Friends, relatives and card club members from Pennington and the surrounding area. *Author's collection.*

scissors from the drawer and choose from an array of roses to be placed in the middle of the dining room table. Card club members would arrive with freshly hot-pressed hair and tasteful outfits complemented by lipstick and jewelry. For some of the card club members, the afternoon was a respite from domestic work, cooking or some other service to a local White family. But card club was the social equalizer, with these service workers enjoying time to sit with Clara the housewife and to savor the opportunity to sip soft drinks, play cards and enjoy one another's company without alcoholic beverages, foul language or the surveillance of employers.

To bring additional income to the family, many married Black women devoted years to the care and service of a White family—even being told they were considered "part of family." Sometimes these ladies who worked as domestics could be readily identified by the surname of the White family for whom they worked. For example, Eva Smith—Fonsie and Clara's sister-in-law—was widely known as the Howe family's domestic worker. Other ladies divided their time between several families or, as an

Alfonso and Clara Smith, circa
1940s. *Author's collection.*

alternative, took in laundry and ironing at home. And many times the relationship between the domestic worker and the employers extended beyond her duties to the family, and a friendship might evolve in spite of America's caste system.

Clara's orderly home routine extended to her food preparation and meal-planning, including careful attention to the canned fruits and vegetables that she would put up seasonally. The cans were arranged on pantry shelves according to whether the contents were a fruit or a vegetable: the two were never mixed on the cellar shelves. And it was not just the food that received her attention; the people to be fed were in her mind too. She canned extra peaches, apricots and pears, favorites of her grandchildren, who frequently had meals at her home. Clara also assigned a special day for washing their everyday clothes, and once dried, the clothes were ironed immediately. While Clara ironed, a grandchild would read articles to her. Clara enjoyed this family tradition, not only because it honed her grandchildren's reading skills but also because she enjoyed speculating about the race of the people reported on in certain articles. Although her discernments went unvalidated, it did not stop her from wondering each time a name was mentioned in an article.

Alfonso and Clara's lives—so disciplined and opinionated—are like William Howe's career and Darlis Maksymovich's memories, emblematic of the variety of experiences, ideas, perspectives, expectations and prejudices that have shaped Pennington and Hopewell communities. This diversity, in turn, is likely a local version of thousands of communities across America.

11

LOOKING BACKWARD

DARLIS MAKSYMOVICH

A 2019 INTERVIEW WITH A RESIDENT OF HOPEWELL, NEW JERSEY: A DESCENDANT OF THE SOUTH CAROLINA BOULWARE FAMILY

I give and bequeath unto my beloved wife, Nancy Boulware, the seven following negroes, namely Matilda and her five children, Judy, Adeline, Archey, Hannah and Charlotte and a young negro woman known by the name of Young Esther, absolutely and forever and at her death to dispose of them according to her own will and pleasure.[82]

When I found the wills of relatives on my maternal grandmother's side of the family in my mother's personal belongings after she passed and began to read them, I was mortified and highly embarrassed. I didn't know what to do. I cried as I realized my family owned slaves. My first reaction was that I threw them across the room. These folks had a lot of slaves—I started counting them, and it was so upsetting to me. I realized I didn't have anything to do with it, but I still find it appalling that anyone had slaves—but to find out your family owned slaves was upsetting and very disconcerting.

I understand it was in the fabric of the nation, and you learn a lot from talking about it. I have only talked about the wills with my son, Elaine and Beverly. I have cousins in New Jersey that I haven't talked to about it. I haven't seen them since my mother's going home service. I think I would talk to them about it now; they're all enlightened. Those of us who were raised in New Jersey come from a different perspective than some of my relatives in South Carolina.

When my mother came to New Jersey in 1938, her oldest sister was already living here. Her two sisters and brother moved up later. Then they all moved back to South Caroline except for my mother. My aunt in South Carolina had a large cotton farm, and she told all of us in New Jersey, "You come back to South Carolina and I will give you ten acres to build a house on; it's yours." That's when three of my relatives moved back to South Carolina.

Growing up, my family went back to South Carolina, and I remember we went for two weeks every summer to visit relatives. I remember seeing signs saying "colored bathroom" and "colored water fountain." Even as a child, I knew it was wrong.

My aunt had two children, and her nanny, Elizabeth, who was a wonderful Black woman, had her daughter handpicked to go to a White school because she was so bright. She was one of the handful of Black children chosen to go to the White school. That's how they desegregated. It was horrible! I believe this was in 1965. Elizabeth was petrified for her daughter, but she didn't have any choice. I was raised in the Princeton area of New Jersey, and I wasn't confronted with any of that, so I didn't understand it.

My mother's oldest brother was a deacon in the church and was very prejudiced. I don't know why my uncle developed this feeling. My father was also a deacon in the church, and he would never ever have that hatred in his heart. I remember when I was sixteen, I got in an argument with my uncle about being so prejudiced and his role as a deacon in the church; that's when my aunt told me to leave her house. She said I was being disrespectful by confronting my uncle. He was a physically large man, and his own children quaked when he spoke, but I was annoyed with him so I wasn't afraid. My aunt told my father, "Get her out of here." So by voicing my opinion to my uncle, his wife asked me to leave because I was being disrespectful to him. I don't know what I said to get the conversation started, but I remember my father putting his arm around me as I was spouting off—and my father politely escorted me out.

To talk about this helps a lot. The wealth of my family was built by the blood, sweat and tears of the enslaved people that our family owned, profited from and passed down from generation to generation. I had learned about slavery in general, but I thought it was just a southern thing. The history is there; we have to acknowledge it.

12

THE PENNINGTON SEMINARY

AN ANCHOR OF "COMMUNITY"

I n 1838, in Washington, D.C., Jesuit priests at what would become Georgetown University sold 272 human beings, in order to secure the future of their institution, which was mired in debt.

"The human cargo was loaded on ships at a bustling wharf in the nation's capital, destined for the plantations of the Deep South. Some slaves pleaded for rosaries as they were rounded up, praying for deliverance." And as babies as young as two months and others were forced to face an unknown fate, their bodies were sacrificed for the 1838 sale which was worth about "$3.3 million in today's dollars."[83]

That same year, in Pennington Borough, the New Jersey Conference of the Methodist Church opened the Pennington Methodist Episcopal Male Seminary with three male students who were promised a "virtuous education,"[84] proudly identified three guiding principles for the education of these three new students: "The education of the physical, the training of the mental, and the grounding of the soul in character.[85] In 1853, when it established a female department, the school was renamed the Pennington Seminary and Female Collegiate Institute.

The Pennington Seminary appears to have had a pattern of hiring local African Americans, many of whom were from the same family. In 1872, Joseph B. Smith, the future father-in-law of Nancy Blackwell, appeared on the payroll ledger of the family or close relatives of an inner circle of Black families who had longtime roots in the region.

A resident of the west side of Scotch Road in Hopewell Township, Joseph—who was descended from enslaved ancestors forced to work without pay—was being well paid for his labor, earning wages averaging $3.00 for a five-day week. By 1882, Smith's pay was up to $3.75 for a week. According to oral history by Lois Geter (Samuel Blackwell's granddaughter), there were also opportunities for what might be called "professional development": the Pennington School encouraged Samuel to improve his math skills since his duties included a weekly trip to Trenton to procure the school's groceries.

George Blackwell, Samuel's son (grandson of Frost), was also employed at the school and was known for his skill in maintaining the lavish garden of the Pennington School headmaster. Pennington School alum Kenneth Anderson wrote,

In the town of Pennington there is a local legend that the compiler of this history has been unable to substantiate, that some of the present Negro families in the town descend from slaves brought north by southern students at the Seminary in order that the students might be helped and watched over in whatever ways the Seminary system and discipline would allow. When the war began, the legend tells, the boys went south; the slaves remained and became free. We are informed by Mrs. Alice B. Blackwell, whose family has lived in or about Pennington since before the Revolution, that slavery was not an unknown or rare institution in New Jersey. In 1834 one of her ancestors, Solomon Titus, left to his wife Susannah, his black woman, Dill. In other old wills of Mrs. Lewis' ancestors in the Pennington area, slaves named Add, Feen, Frey and Dinah are mentioned. In 1819—we learn from an old account book—Black Cadis ran away. With the coming of the Civil War, white men of Pennington Town built a number of little houses on South Main Street for the colored families to rent. Most of them worked for their former masters or other white people. In 1938, Pennington Seminary celebrated its Centennial. Many distinguished speakers visited the campus and took part in a three-day commemoration. "Uncle" George Blackwell, Dr. Green's aged Negro gardener, religiously and in fine attire attended the various meetings.[86]

This "Uncle" George Blackwell was described as a short man. Old-timers interviewed for the *Princeton Recollector* in the mid-1970s recalled,

George Blackwell, I would say, was not over 5'1" and he was sort of broad. He was a very religious man, but he was comical. He always had a

joke. He was a local preacher, and he'd reach here when the minister didn't preach. He was a member of the Methodist Church in Pennington. When they took up the collection (at the Camp Meetings), someone would holler to Uncle George Blackwell, "I'll give you a dollar if you sing that 'They Stole My Mother Away.'" He went around through the gang with a plate a-singing. You see this old man, George Blackwell, he's the one they wanted to hear sing this. And people used to come from miles to hear him sing it. They'd start waving dollar bills. He'd sing some songs, but he wouldn't sing that one. He'd save it til the last so he could get some money for the minister that preached. They were dying to hear him sing that one. And he was a great singer. They were crazy about that.[87]

13

LOOKING BACKWARD

THE VAN LIEU FAMILY MAY 10, 2021 INTERVIEW

"LOOKING WITH FRESH EYES"

The world that early New Jersey dwellers made was a world from which—to use the biblical phrase—"the sins of our fathers" have left pain from which everyone, Black and White, now needs to heal. It is not uncommon for White people to express confusion, shame and guilt, particularly after gaining awareness of the inhumane ways their ancestors ostracized and otherwise inflicted violence on Black and Brown community members. Many twenty-first-century New Jersey dwellers are now seeking concrete ways to make a better, more tolerant and less violent world for themselves and their descendants.

Family secrets can cause some folks to go through a myriad of emotions, which some have described as "distressing," "embarrassing," "gut wrenching" and "shocking." These were some of the emotions identified by a family who agreed to be interviewed via Zoom during the summer of 2021.

"My brother, sister and I debated about giving it [the interview] anonymously. My sister feels that we should not deny the stain, while I am concerned with creating an association with the Klan and current family members who may still live in the region." The family's final decision was to use their voice in the hope that others, who may go through a similar experience of uncovering an ugly family secret, would find the courage to speak their truth so the process of healing could begin through their words.

When the email arrived on a spring day in April 2021, the writer identified himself with an introduction that came quickly to the point:

Dear authors, my sister just presented me with a copy of "If These Stones Could Talk," which I immediately read. It has had a profound effect. Reading so many names that we share was a revelation. My family lived in the area for many generations, my grandfather and father being born in Hopewell. There was a farm on Back Brook Road in the family since before the Revolution until the 50's. My mother and father went to Pennington High, I think he was in the class of '39, possibly '41 or near. Everything I read resounded, but with a new tone. I am taken aback by my ignorance. To think for all of my nearly seventy years that slavery was a "southern thing." Whippings in Flemington? Coincidentally, during my sister's visit, we dug through some boxes and found a despicable work, "The Ku Klux Klan in Prophecy," which most likely belonged to one of my great uncles. Your book tells us that the Klan was a significant presence in Hunterdon County, not just a few outliers. This was an eye opener. Your work should be in curricula nationwide. I am now eager to go back to New Jersey to visit the sites you mention, and to look at the land of our ancestors with fresh eyes. Thank you for what you have taught me. I look for more.

A couple of months later, this family—consisting of two brothers and their sister—told their story:

I was about seven years old. The KKK was in our family, and some of us did know it. We were small children in the backseat of our car, and our parents mentioned a cross burning. Our great-uncle had participated in the cross burning, and as kids we questioned why. I remember Dad toning things down to make it sound like "just a club" and that our great-uncle needed something to do with the "boys" and that they really didn't mean anything by it. That's all I remember about participation by a family member. I don't know how the papers got into our father's possession. I can only speculate that Dad got them from his father's papers; he was his father's brother and all were from the Sourland Mountain region. I refuse to honor the claim that it was just a club or something to do after work the way our father explained it.

When I first saw the photo of the march from 1922 or 1923, around ten or fifteen years ago, I learned about this. Dad told me which uncle it was. If it was more than one in Washington [referring to the Klan march], we just don't know. Knowing photos were there, I hoped he had just happened to be in Washington when those photos were taken, but the Alma White book takes care of that idea. A cross burning during our lifetime is particularly close, and it's quite shocking to me. What I have learned in the last few years is that all of these issues are so close; they are not in the distant past, as I had assumed all my life that this was something that happened a long time ago. It's all been a shocking revelation to me, and I regret it has taken me sixty-five years or so to start to see some of this. It's now for so many people; it's now.

After reading excerpts from the Alma White book, I realized this was part of the Alma White mythology or ideology. Zarapath was where the Alma White church was. They had a radio show and a big church, and it's not that far from where we lived in Hopewell. There's no mistaking the message. It's complicated; our parents considered themselves to be tolerant, and they wanted to raise us to be tolerant. We grew up with a vague understanding of tolerance and bigotry. As children, it's hard to grasp, so it's entirely possible our parents didn't want us to know there were people in the family who ascribed to bigotry and hatred. Hunterdon County is hugely conservative.

Mother was eastern European and was born in the States. This was a step too far for our grandfather. Our family is seriously intermarried with a handful of families going back to the Revolution. We are also direct descendants of John Hart and Penelope VanPrincis. It's worth mentioning it was a big deal for our father to marry our mother, especially in the context of the Alma White book that Blacks, Jews and Catholics will destroy America. Our mother was Catholic and eastern European. According to our maternal grandparents' immigration records from Ellis Island and our mother's racial category, according to the immigration record it was Magyar, which means not White; it's a variant. In some circles, it was tantamount to an interracial marriage because racial categories in the early twentieth century were different—like the English and Irish were not ethnicities. There's something about our parents wanting to raise more tolerant children because they, themselves, had objections from our grandparents. When they married, our paternal grandfather said our father marrying into our mother's family was like a rose in a dung heap.

If These Stones Could Talk is really fascinating because there are so many names in that book that are in our family. There is not a clear understanding at all how the families were related. Our family history was compiled in the 1950s, which traced our family in the States back to about 1670. One of the earliest documents is a will where one of our founding family relatives bequeathed her slaves to her children. They were Dutch, and she wrote, "These slaves can choose which children they want to go live with." In this book about our family history at the bottom of page six there's a paragraph that is titled "Negroes Who Bear Our Name," and it's the only mention of it. It read, "Our ancestors on Long Island and especially those in New Jersey were slave owners like other people of means. When those slaves were freed a number of them adopted the surname of their former owners having no surname of their own. We are informed this was a compliment for those who were maltreated and were not interested in ever again hearing their owner's name. There are thus a number of Negro Van Lieus and Van Lieu families living in Newark, New Brunswick and Galveston, Texas. Almost every old Dutch, English and French Huguenot family name is represented by the Negroes in America." That is the sum total of what he wrote.

We knew there were members of the family who were enslaved and never knew who they were or what happened to them. Clark is a family name; Truehart is a family name as well as Hoagland and Blackwell. We also know John Hart had slaves, and I strongly suspect the White Blackwell family and Black Blackwell families are related by blood. There are so many common names that this experience is extremely intense.

Growing up in Hunterdon County, we didn't know any Black people, and there were no Black people in our social life. We never saw them when we went to town or church. Our entire world was White. It was almost like a kind of a mythology that there were Black people or there used to be Black people in the way we were viewing the world then. So, part of the intensity I am feeling is discovering how completely utterly wrong that is and that there's a whole entire world we never knew existed, let alone understand it or be in it. Our grandfather had a construction business in Flemington, New Jersey. We have some family home movies that my father took on the job because he liked to document his work on the job. There was a Black man with a wheelbarrow in one of these films who was referred to as either "Brownie" or "Blackie." I can't remember which, but that was how he was known to the crew on the job, the only Black person on the job. And then on my mother's side, they had a farm and they had tenant farmers and one was Black. Once in a while, the tenant would come to the back door to talk to my grandfather about business, but he was never allowed inside. And he was also either "Blackie" or "Brownie." They were the only two Black people we had ever encountered until high school.

I recall one time when the tenant farmer did come; he had a little son about my age, and my mother directed me to play with this kid. And we played in the dirt in the driveway. It was like a curious sense of knowing what was right and wrong on her part and trying to do something right. That may have been my first actual contact with a Black person, and there was nothing meaningful until later on in school. We went to a pretty tony prep school, and there were Black men who worked in the kitchen. And it may have been the first indication of the systematic and subtle racism in the fact that they only had first names and no last names. I am embarrassed and regretful to think of what I have learned only in the last few years. I will be seventy years old in July, and I realized about five years ago when I would drive to work and would think *I wish this person ahead of me would go a little faster so I can get to work.* Then I realized that if the driver of that vehicle is Black or Hispanic, they could go five miles over the limit and get pulled over and I wouldn't. It was such a realization that it was one of the daily obstacles and indignities I'm surrounded by.

From my young days, I recall I was working for someone whose car needed servicing, so I took it to a garage in Jamesburg. The serviceman told me this hilarious anecdote about a Black family who came interested in purchasing a car. When he found out they had the same last name as the owner he thought it was just hilarious because they were Black, almost like they had absconded with the name. He did not find it honorable they had the same last name and was telling me this like I was also supposed to find it hilarious. In those days, I was

Hopewell Herald, February 6, 1924

There was a spectacular showing of fiery crosses surrounding Hopewell last Friday evening, starting about 9 o'clock. The burning lasted for about two hours. They were placed near the reservoir to the north, at the top of Crusher's hill to the east, on the hill near Mount Rose to the south, and near the old stone crusher to the west. It is supposed that they were symbols of the Ku Klux Klan organization. It is said that were 100 crosses burned that night throughout Mercer County, in practically every section.

Hopewell Herald article from 1924 on cross burnings in the Hopewell area. *Author's collection.*

impassive and didn't respond to things like that for years and years and let it wash over me. That was one of the first times I heard about the interconnection with the families, and I cannot imagine that we are not related by blood.

LOOKING BACKWARD

MEGHAN SPEAKS
AT HER DECEMBER 20, 2020 INTERVIEW

Meghan, in her early thirties at the time of this interview, grew up in Hunterdon County. In 2018, she attended a presentation by Elaine Buck and Beverly Mills titled "A Proud Heritage," which was based on *If These Stones Could Talk*. Following the presentation, Meghan hesitantly approached the authors but was unable to utter a word. Instead, she burst into tears. Through her embarrassment, Meghan confessed that her tears were the result of a horrible discovery she had made as she sorted through family artifacts: a census record listing two African American children and a letter from one ancestor to another describing slaveholding, both of which indicated that her family once held slaves as part of their labor force. The African Americans listed in the census most likely were serving her ancestors under the terms of New Jersey's 1804 Gradual Abolition Act, which granted freedom to any child born to a slave after July 4, 1804, but required these children to serve their mother's owner until age twenty-five if male and twenty-one if female.[88] This is Meghan's story:

> I didn't grow up on the farm like much of my family did, but always had good memories surrounding it. Family picnics, apple pies, a positive feeling of family history in the land. I always knew that my family had deep ties to the Hillsborough area; we can trace our family back to the *Mayflower*, and thinking back I always felt

proud and happy about that. Our family attended South Branch Dutch Reformed Church, which always provided a welcoming environment. Even today, from far away, I can almost smell the church sanctuary when I imagine it. As children, we would explore the building and sneak up to the balcony. I never gave much thought to why there was a balcony in the first place.

I studied cultural geography in college, which is about where you live and the connections people have to places. I would say my connection to the farm was, and very much before I attended the presentation, considered ideal. Today my view of the farm might be different from my cousins who grew up on it. My aunts and uncles all worked on it together and may have more of a personal relationship in terms of their memories of the farm.

The letter that I found was from my grandmother's family, many generations back. Excerpts from the document include the following:

William Craig, father of Robert, had slaves among whom was one, Reuben. William could not see well and started to boss the work hands. They would slip away under the trees. Another slave was Pierrie Craig. The slaves were brought in ship loads from New Guinea—a strange business. They were often the size of giants, as was Pierrie. Some people raised their own slaves, and others would buy from them. I do not know if William raised his own. Boss Craig gave the niggers a day off at Christmas and they decided to "bump" a little rum but they didn't get any. On New Yrs. day they were free. One said, "Give me a drink of rum or I'll ———. Boss Craig would pick up a pole and wack [sic] him over the neck. "Tune" Melick had slaves you inherited. These could not be turned loose, but had to go through papers even when set free, but some ran away and went South. Papers were called "manuensis [sic]" papers. When William Craig's were freed they went to Somerville and lived in the better of two sections for Negroes. One, Charlie Craig, worked for Davenports and drove on top of a carriage; later he was a janitor of St. John's Church. Charlie had a daughter (and a son) who married a minister. Nancy worked for Miss Cammon (Miss Otis' friend). There were several other girls, one of whom worked for Miss Otis' mother occasionally as a cook. All were good cooks. She would make Miss Otis a molasses pie when pie fillings ran out. The girls didn't like Charlie's wife. On one occasion, when they thought she was high hat, they spanked her. William Craig gave each daughter a slave. Mary Craig Lane's was Myra, Agnes was Reuben's daughter. Gertrude Potter had one also, Elizabeth Craig Conover.

My grandmother moved to the farm when she and my grandfather got married. They took ownership of the land around 1910–12. It was a gift from my great-grandfather, who gave it to my grandfather.

When we talk about white privilege today, I'm sure that there are members of my family who would say we are not privileged because we have always had to work hard for what we have. As a family, we do not have endless money, and things haven't always come easily—in fact, most things have been a challenge. However, to me the privilege is that I could make it until my twenties and thirties without wondering who my ancestors were or what job they had; it was privilege that made me assume that because we lived in New Jersey, the North, that slavery wasn't part of my family's history. Privilege is what allows our community to ignore the past and use their own personal fortitude to justify historic atrocities.

After your talk at the library, I subscribed to Ancestry.com and dug into the 1800s census records of my family. In the 1830 census, I found one African American on the property, an eleven-year-old boy named Peter Peterson. A woman named Diaw Peterson and her two-year-old, Harriet, were listed under a family on a nearby property's record; my assumption is that Diaw was Peter's mom. In the 1860 census, Peter was listed as a farm laborer at age twenty-one, and another African American, Jane Vanderveer, was listed as a servant. Jane was only a teenager. I tried to follow Peter, to see where he might have ended up and where his descendants may now be living. I found a Civil War record for him but no further information after that.

Now when I think about our farmland and the land in the Hillsborough area, I look at everything differently. I wonder where Peter would have stayed and how it was for an eleven-year-old child working and living there alone. I also thought about the church history and the balcony. An older church member once remarked that when the parishioners worshipped, they would bring their slaves, who would be sent to the balcony, where they were sometimes shackled.

It's hard to know where to go from here, knowing what I now know. My family made choices in the 1860s that were not mine, but I still feel like I haven't done enough. My privilege is that I have not had to think about the choices of my ancestors unto now. George Floyd was just murdered, and it made me realize that my six-year-old son doesn't have to think about his race. How do I raise my children to make sure they understand their family's history, to ensure they can recognize their own privilege where it exists and take action to be advocates for justice in spite of the choices their ancestors made? I remember when I told my one family member that I planned to attend your presentation, she asked me, "Why would you want to do that?"

15

LOOKING BACKWARD

PEG VAN HISE, MEMBER OF
THE PENNINGTON HIGH SCHOOL CLASS OF 1941,
SPEAKS EIGHTY YEARS LATER

In the chapter titled "African American History Is American History" in *If These Stones Could Talk*, a story about William Smith's travels to Washington, D.C., with his fellow students on their senior class trip in 1941 was recounted. The most important destination, as described by the student writer, was the Hotel Continental, where "our first thought was to get a few minutes rest and to become acquainted with our new surroundings, and then on to dinner in the Continental Room of the Hotel."

One of the ninety-two graduates from the class of 1941, Margaret "Peg" Van Hise, was ninety-eight years old and remembered the trip well. She also remembered that William Smith, the great-grandson of Joseph Smith, always went by the nickname "Shud." Peg was still wondering why. While Shud lived his seventy years identifying by this nickname, one thing that people could agree on was that no one could pin down the origin of the nickname. In the yearbook, across Peg's class picture, she wrote to Shud, "Two things I'll never forget 1. The 'hot-foot' in Chemistry class, 2. Your basketball. Keep up the good work, Peg." John Morgan Van Hise, Peg's future husband and teammate, wrote, "Hi Shud, Best of everything to a swell pal. You sure have been a good sport," Hise. Whatever the meaning of the nickname, however, Peg remembered her friendship with her classmate Shud.

But Peg also remembered the class trip to Washington, and she continues to wish that she had defended and stood up for her friend in a reprehensible situation. From May 15 through the 17, the class enjoyed sightseeing tours of the city, strolls along Pennsylvania Avenue after dinner and ate delicious meals in the Continental Room. And so the last entry recorded in the yearbook about the trip read, "And so ninety-two students and five chaperones, all very tired and worn out from the three exciting days that we had spent on our trip to Washington arrived home at last at approximately 10:00 Saturday evening with many pleasant memories to ponder over for some time to come."

Eighty years later, Peg recalled a memory from that senior class trip that still troubled her, and she wanted to talk about it, as she had in the past with her family. One chilly fall afternoon, Peg shared these words as she sat on her sofa in the apartment where she lived in an assisted living facility:

> Your father always went through school by the nickname "Shud." My husband, Morgan, went to his funeral at the church right across from the old primary school. Shud was very close to my husband when they were in high school. He played sports, soccer and baseball. I'm not sure if he played basketball because he was kind of short, but he played all the sports with my husband, Morgan Van Hise.
>
> Pennington was a great place to grow up; there were nine kids in our family, a bunch of us. We all went to the local schools, and my maiden name was Miller. My father and mother moved there in 1915 from Trenton. My father had a business school in Indiana along with his brother-in-law, but they weren't making enough money. They applied to Rider College for jobs, and my father taught penmanship and stenography. There were three Miller families in Pennington, a family on Main Street and another family across from the high school. I would walk up the railroad tracks or hitchhike to go to Hopewell to the quarry to swim. I used to watch Doris Baldwin swim because she was a beautiful swimmer, and I would try to imitate her. Later, I spent my adult years as a swimming instructor. I learned to love swimming from the quarry.
>
> I remember the Clark family who lived on Dublin Road because Mr. Clark would walk across the fields, across the railroad tracks, up my father's driveway on Welling Avenue to Main Street to get the bus to Trenton. As kids, when we would come in all dirty and muddy, my father would say, "You been playing with Mr. Clark's family," which was my father's idea of humor. We would see Mr.

Clark up and down the driveway every day. Our families did intermingle sort of, but not much. We met the children (meaning African Americans) when we were older in school in our classes; that was all. The churches were different, although the AME started the Pennington group of churches and were quite active.

I knew your father was the only Black person on the class trip to Washington. We went on the train, and I'm sure your father was on the train but he could not stay in the hotel. They dropped us at the hotel, and then they would take him to where he was staying. The next morning, they would pick him up and bring him to the hotel to be with us. I'll never forget he was there on the Washington trip with us, and what bothers me is that none of us spoke up. No, we did not. I don't care, although we couldn't have done anything about it, we could have made our voice heard, but we did not. So, trying to make up for it now it's kind of late.

Looking back, I remember your father came dressed up in a suit, and he looked just like all the others. What I remember is that we didn't say anything, and that's what bothers me. So that was the way it was. I don't remember where he sat on the train, probably with the guys who played sports. If he was close to anybody, it was them. I know he was my husband's very good friend, but they didn't go out socially together. But they rode on the team bus to the basketball games together, and he did go with them then because they needed him. But outside of school no socialization took place.

We never talked about race at home. We had nine kids in my family, and we never talked about it. My father grew up in a medium-sized family and grew up in the East. He was very religious and was always busy with the Methodist church on the board and as a Sunday school teacher. He sent us all to college, and not all of us finished—but we had the opportunity. He took us to Radio City every Christmas. And even though he was religious, we never talked about integration.

I used to see Mr. Clark walk up our driveway, but other than that there weren't a lot of Blacks around. At school, there weren't many in our classes, and in my class, it was two, and one was your father, but we could've spoken up. Well, it was a good place to grow up, anyway.

16

HENRY BALLARD CLARK

A SEVENTH SON MIGRATES FROM VIRGINIA

H enry Ballard Clark, known as Ballard, was the seventh son born to Henry and Louisa Morehead in Gretna, Virginia. It was 1873, and the end of Reconstruction was looming. A mere four years later, federal troops would be withdrawn from the former Confederate States of America, and many of the gains realized by Black America for a little over a decade would be all but erased. The Freedmen's Bureau, created shortly before the end of the Civil War, offered African Americans a glimmer of hope as they attempted assimilation into a society that found it hard to envision them as human beings. Henry Louis Gates Jr. noted,

> *In the broadest terms, Reconstruction was a revolutionary time in American life—a time of national renewal extended out from four years of Civil War, death, and destruction that narrowed the gap between the country's ideals and laws and advanced racial progress. Yet it was also a turbulent and brutally violent period, one marked by rapid economic change and new forms of white resistance that included everything from organized paramilitary assaults and political assassination to night rides and domestic terror.*[89]

For years, historians have offered various explanations of why Reconstruction failed. Many of these explanations centered on the economy and the resurgence of White southern Democrat power, as well as a plethora of state and federal legal decisions by judges and legislators who leaped at the chance to challenge rights gained by Blacks. Noted historian Eric Foner explained it this way:

Reconstruction provided space for the creation of key institutions of Black America—the independent church, schools and colleges, and stable families, which became the springboards for future struggle. It's [state] *laws and Constitutional amendments* [the Thirteenth, Fourteenth and Fifteenth] *remained on the books ensuring that the Jim Crow system that followed, at least as a matter of law, remained a regional, not a national system.*[90]

Regardless of the success or failure of Reconstruction, Black people desired to own farms, homes in which to raise families and opportunities to build legacies that they could pass down to their descendants—the same desires White people had.

Ballard Clark, wanting to be a property owner, left the little hamlet of Gretna in the early 1890s, headed for New Jersey. There he worked as a farm laborer, while his fiancée, Pinky Coles, stayed behind in the neighboring town of Chatham, Virginia. Pinky, the daughter of Milton and Susie Belle Coles, who had been enslaved, awaited Ballard's visits and planned to join her beloved to lay down roots in New Jersey. The couple, each just twenty-two years old, was married on January 1, 1896, at the Smith Field Church in Pittsylvania County, Virginia. Then they made their way to New Jersey, where they rented a house near Pennington and began raising a family that grew to twelve children, nine of whom survived to adulthood. Eventually, Ballard and Pinky were able to buy a plot of land and establish a subsistence farm, feeding their large family with fruits, vegetables, chickens, hogs and cows.

Ballard's exemplary work ethic was reflected in his children, who watched him leave the house each morning, regardless of the weather, to go to his job at the Essex Rubber Mill in Trenton. Leaving his back door, he would cut across the field for about half a mile before he reached the highway, which he crossed, before cutting down the private driveways of some of the towns' White families. A Mercer County historian has described the industry in an internet history of the community:

The rubber industry began in 1850 with Jonathan H. Green's plant. Another early pioneer of the industry was Alan Magowan and his son, Frank. In 1868 they converted the Whitehead factory into the Whitehead Brothers Rubber Company. It was built in 1870, and is said to be the oldest rubber mill in the United States. Trenton was also "the nation's tire capital" at one point. The car's popularity after 1900 encouraged most of

MARRIAGE LICENSE

Virginia, Pittsylvania Co. to-wit:

TO ANY PERSON LICENSED TO CELEBRATE MARRIAGES:

You are hereby authorized to join together in the Holy State of Matrimony according to the rites and ceremonies of your Church, or religious denomination, and the laws of the Commonwealth of Virginia,

BALLARD CLARK

AND   PINKEY COLES

Given under my hand as Clerk of the County Court of Pittsylvania this __30"__ day of __December__ 18 9_. .

W. B. Shepherd   CLERK

Certificate to obtain a marriage license.
To be Annexed to the License, required by Section 2229 of the Code of Virginia.

Time of Marriage __1st. January 1896__ Place of Husband's Birth __Pittsylvania__

Place of Marriage __-----__ Place of Wife's Birth __ "__

Full Names of Parties Married Ballard Place of Husband's Residence __ "__
Clark and Pinkey Coles

Place of Wife's Residence __ "__

Color __Col'd.__

Age of Husband __22__ Names of Husband's Parents __Henry(Dec'd__

and Louisa Clark

Age of Wife __22__

Condition of Husband (widowed or single) __Single__ Names of Wife's Parents __Milton and__

Belle Coles

Condition of Wife(widowed or single) __Single__ Occupation of Husband __Farm Hand__

Given under my hand this 30" December 1895. W. B. Shepherd, Clerk.

MINISTER'S RETURN OF MARRIAGE

I Certify, That on the __1st__ day of __January__ 1896 at __Smith Field__
Church united in Marriage the above-named and described parties, under authority of the annexed License.

Rev. D. Keen

A Copy Teste: CLERK

Oct. 31 1940

Copy of 1896 marriage license of Henry Ballard Clark and Pinky Coles. *Author's collection.*

Trenton's rubber factories—and there were many—to make tires. However, Trenton reached the peak of its rubber production while manufacturing materials for World War I. At one point, there were eighteen rubber companies in Mercer County.[91]

So Ballard had landed in a lucrative industrial region. But when Ballard wasn't working in Trenton, he augmented his income as the "handyman" to Percy Sked, one of five sons of the Sked family. Percy, an entrepreneurial man, was known as a cattle dealer, farmer and real estate owner. As noted by the *Trenton Times*,

Percy Sked is quite a business person for one who has not reached the age of manhood. Last week he purchased a fine bull at William Leigh's sale and killed it at his home, dressed it and took it to Trenton and sold it. It tipped the scales at 423 pounds.[92]

The relationship between Ballard and Percy Sked lasted for many years, and the model entrepreneurship and hard work influenced the nine Clark children. Some started their own businesses and/or served in the military. Son Guyfred died from inhaling toxic fumes from his factory job, where he had worked double shifts. The eldest son, Irving, a World War I veteran, joined more than seventy citizens from the Pennington region who fought in this war—only to come home to segregated welcome-home celebrations.

When World War I ended in victory for the allies, Pennington celebrated the November 11, 1918 signing of the Armistice with much gaiety, bell ringing, and a parade. The parade was composed of the children of the Academy Street School, the students of the Seminary, and townspeople.

On September 20, 1919, the town again honored its brave soldiers who had returned from war. There was a catered affair at the Pennington Prep School, speeches by the mayor and other dignitaries and thousands of dahlias sent by former mayor William P. Howe Sr. to be distributed. The event was extravagant:

The Hildebrecht Catering Company supplied the dinner which included oysters on the half shell, sweet pickles, olives, cream of tomato soup, saltines, rolls, filet of sole, potatoes marguerite, roast young chicken, glace sweet potatoes, green peas, tomato and lettuce salad, French dressing, ice

cream bricks, fancy cakes, coffee, cigars, and cigarettes. Although the repast was received with much relish and enthusiasm, one of the most touching features of the evening was the service of the eight colored men who waited on the tables. Having known most of these boys all their lives, they had volunteered to serve the banquet. Mutual respect and gratitude on the parts of both groups were so evident that it would have been difficult to state which was more pleased. A Trenton orchestra provided music, a professional entertainer presented a program, and all joined in singing such popular favorites of the period as "Peg O' My Heart," "O How I Hate to Get Up in the Morning," "K-K-K Katy," "Pack Up Your Troubles in Your Old Kit Bag," "Swanee," "Keep the Home Fires Burning," "Over There," and "It's a Long Long Way to Tipperary." Iced sherbet was dispensed from booths throughout the entire evening and at ten o'clock, young girls, dressed in white and wearing arm bands of the national colors—served cake and ice cream to all. The evening ended with dancing.

But Pennington's Black war hero was celebrated at a separate event:

After the banquet, Mayor Clarkson and Committee members, E.B. Knowles and George Scarborough, formed an honor guard to escort Irving Clark to the Odd Fellows Hall. As the only negro boy of the town in service, his race was anxious to hold a special reception as a tribute to him. About 150 were present at this event which was marked by a program of entertainment that had been arranged by the Reverends Groves and Jones of the Baptist and AME Churches. Brief addresses were delivered by the three members of the guard of young Clark. Refreshments included ice cream, sherbet and cake.[93]

Despite the disrespect the family faced for their contribution to their country's safety, the Ballards remained in Pennington and continued to thrive. During World Word II, the youngest Clark sibling, Arthur (who went by Dick), was off to war, representing his family's commitment to "freedom" and justice. Ballard's oldest daughters, Clara and Rose, became the area's first Black women business owners—Clara with a candy store and Rose with a hair salon. Baby sister Marvel graduated from Pennington High School with high honors. Though she was accepted at Douglas College, Depression-era economics made it impossible for her family to send her there.

Throughout the years, grandchildren and great-grandchildren were familiar with the name Percy Sked and the story of how the family became owners of the homestead on Dublin Road. Although it's highly likely, but

Fiftieth wedding anniversary of Ballard and Pinky Clark (*center*). Pictured here also are daughters Rose Caffee (*top left*), Clara Smith (*left*) and Frieda Taylor (*right*). *Author's collection.*

not documented that Percy also owned the house directly across the street, Ballard's youngest child, Arthur, purchased that property, where he raised a family of six along with his wife, Winifred. The enterprising spirit was not lost on Dick, who eventually started his own landscaping business from knowledge gained from his employment with Howe Nurseries. For decades, the two Clark families remained the only Black residents on Dublin Road until the mid-1960s, when another Black family became homeowners, which finally boosted the number to three.

A CASTLE BUILT ON HATE...AND A GRAVE OF A CIVIL RIGHTS ICON

In 1876, Webster Edgerly, a self-proclaimed health guru, began to gain fame and fortune by creating an organization called the Ralston Health Club, which was built on seven principles to live by: "activity, light, strength, temperature, oxygen and nature." Edgerly then began to expand his organization and establish a community that would share in his belief system. Apparently, he came to the right place. Located in Hopewell Borough on Greenwood Avenue across from the Highland Cemetery, the Ralston Health Club purportedly attracted as many as "800,000 members, including several former American Presidents, and supposedly, Queen Victoria herself."[94] By 1902, the cult-like organization had become so popular that "Purina Mills founder, William Danforth, paid Edgerly to endorse his company's cereal products, going so far as to enter a partnership with Edgerly and change the name of his company to Ralston Purina."[95] The Ralston Purina organization, with its offices and plant located in St. Louis, Missouri, continued operations until it was purchased by the Nestlé Corporation in 2001.

Edgerly, who wrote under the pen name of Edmund Shaftesbury, authored numerous publications, including books that were devoid of facts or science, instead leaning on beliefs that were steeped in racism. He recommended special exercises, bizarre body movements and strict dietary regimes, which he believed were all part of building a human race that "should be strictly Caucasian because nature, the Bible, history and science speak plainly and conclusively on this question."[96] Also central to Edgerly's belief system was the castration of Black men, to prevent them from passing along what he described as inferior intellectual capacity. Logically, however, Edgerly did not object to White male men mating with Black women, since he believed that the intellect of the mother would not be passed to offspring.

While Hopewell's Black community continued to flourish, Edgerly was busily planning to purchase large tracts of farmland on a ridge outside of town where he would create an invitingly designed community where this new improved White race would reside. Surrounding his own spacious twenty-seven-thousand-square-foot Victorian home, Edgerly planted expensive Norwegian spruce and ginkgo trees from China. And by 1894, he had begun laying out a plan for four hundred homes, small farms; five other large estates—mirroring his own—would be available to a few wealthy White families.

At first, many Hopewell citizens were dazzled by Edgerly's swagger and boldness. But soon some local residents began to suspect he intended to take over the region and use it for his own gain. The local distrust increased after Edgerly began spreading alarm that the region was in danger of being destroyed by fire, then "solved" the problem by building a faulty reservoir. Subsequently, he was only able to buy twenty-five of the four hundred lots in his White-only town. Edgerly and his wife moved to Trenton, New Jersey, where he died at age seventy-four in 1926. The Ralston Health Club died with him. Though Edgerly's Hopewell plans failed, his legacy remains in Hopewell Borough through street names that all harken back to the Ralston philosophy: Grandview, Ralston, Eastern, North Star, Sunrise and Shaftesbury, the surname of his writing alias, Edmund Shaftsbury.[97]

During the same years that Edgerly was conceiving that his master race community would overtake Hopewell, William Ashby was a young boy growing up in Newport News, Virginia. There, at the age of eleven, he witnessed the remains of a man he knew hanging from a sycamore tree—the victim of a lynching. Seeing the victim's open mouth with its tongue grotesquely displayed, Ashby remembered, years later, that his own young mind wondered if perhaps the victim "was asking why he was tortured and murdered."[98]

Witnessing the horror of lynching changed the life of young William Mobile Ashby, who was born in 1889 in Carter's Grove, Virginia. So, too, did he know that his own grandfather had been beaten to death and had his throat slashed by a White mob acting out their resentment because of his economic success. William Ashby's family relocated to Newport News, Virginia, and subsequently, Ashby and his mother left Virginia for New Jersey, where the young Ashby worked as a gardener and waiter before attending Lincoln University, where he completed his undergraduate degree in 1911—

Hopewell Castle. *Courtesy of Zillow.com.*

four years before U.S. president Woodrow Wilson, a former president of the nearby Princeton University lauded the race hatred–based Ku Klux Klan by airing the film *Birth of a Nation* in the White House and by praising the film as "history written with lightning."[99] The consequent emboldening of the KKK could not have been lost on Ashby as he went on to earn a divinity degree from Yale University in 1916 and accepted a position as director of the Newark Urban League, from which he launched an illustrious career that led him to be recognized as the state's first Black social worker.

William Ashby, who dedicated his professional life to social work and social justice, was known throughout the state. His tie to Hopewell, though, was through his wife, Mary Arnold, a descendant of a Black Revolutionary War veteran, William Stives, whose family was the first free Black family to settle on the Sourland Mountain. Late in his life, Ashby remembered meeting Mary at a dance in Plainfield, New Jersey:

> *There glided past me a sylph, a sprite, She was dressed in blue and wore high-button shoes. Her dark brown hair fell loosely over her shoulders, and ended almost at her waist. She laughed. It had all the happiness of the song of a lark at the first rays of daylight. I met her. Her name was Mary Arnold and she was from Hopewell, New Jersey. She has been with me ever since.*[100]

Right: William Ashby. *Courtesy of Theodora Ashby*.

Below: William and Mary Ashby and family at birthday celebration. *Courtesy of Theodora Ashby*.

William Asbhy—community leader, fighter of racism and promoter of civil rights—was dedicated to social, economic and environmental justice and was recognized for his years of commitment to these causes. Recounting his life story in his autobiography, *Tales Without Hate*, he left a legacy that was honored by numerous organizations, commissions and political figures. Ashby, founder of the Urban League branches in Elizabeth and Newark (where a monument has been erected in his memory), was also recognized for his leadership in Trenton, where the Department of Community Affairs renamed the building in his honor. Some of his admirers are planning a memorial to Ashby to be erected in Washington, D.C.

Having dedicated more than nine decades of his life fighting for human rights and equality for all citizens, Ashby died in 1991 at age 101, three years after his beloved wife, Mary, and almost a half century after their only child, Catherine.

He was laid to rest beside his wife in the Highland Cemetery in Hopewell, which is situated directly across the street from Webster Edgerly's castle—a mansion built on hatred and greed.

Two men, Edgerly and Ashby, with opposing views of humanity: both had ties to Hopewell that have left an unforgettable mark on the region's history.

18

THE VOICE OF ELAINE BUCK

PERSONAL REFLECTIONS ON RACE AND THE LONG LEGACY OF THE AFRICAN AMERICAN STRUGGLE

I t's been almost seven decades since I've lived as an African American woman in the United States. History has never been interesting to me, and I often tell the story of how I was asked to leave my high school history class after I questioned why there was such a lack of information about African Americans and their accomplishments in our history books. Why were there only pictures of old, ugly White men with bad wigs?

When I look at the work of one of our most revered local historians, Alice Lewis Blackwell, author of *Hopewell Valley Heritage* (1973), I actually marvel at how the author meticulously researched and memorialized the families and backgrounds of the region's founding White families. For an African American, it has been a resource to help trace the history of people who owned the ancestors of people who live on my block, went to church with, attended school with, socialized with and even married. Attempts to trace my African American ancestral roots in Hopewell Valley have been frustrating, leaving me with more questions than answers. My tireless efforts working to uplift the memory of our ancestors has only been met by repeated dead ends, roadblocks and lack of information, which has encouraged me to dig deeper into the history of what was then Hunterdon County's early Black presence.

My family fled the South and came north because of racial violence, lynching, trauma and socioeconomic disparities. I have heard the oral histories my family has told about their sacrifices of being separated from their loved ones left behind and scattered all over the country during slavery. I think about how my family was among the legions of African Americans who lived through enslavement, Reconstruction, Jim Crow and the Great Migration. I've heard the story of how my family traveled North through the Blue Ridge Mountains, which can be as dark as a thousand midnights in a cypress swamp at night. I learned they had to find a place to relieve themselves, to rest and refresh themselves fearing the unknown at all times. I learned how they traveled through the many "sundown towns" positioned across America where African Americans were legally barred from accommodations and were forced to find establishments that would serve African Americans for lodging, food, gas and using the restrooms.

My family's story began in the early 1940s and 1950s, when my uncle John Jones had an old work truck that he used to make runs from Skillman, New Jersey, to Danville, Virginia, to pick up friends and relatives to bring them North to work. Some were fleeing the threat of lynching or some other brutal form of punishment. The passengers would sit in the truck bed, packed with belongings and prepared food such as fried chicken, biscuits and boiled eggs and canned peaches—foods that traveled well without coolers. Their most important belonging would be their Bible. Uncle John had a tarp in case the weather was bad or if he had to hide the people from the watchful eye of the White patrollers, some of whom were self-appointed and accustomed to policing the movement of Black people—a custom that dates back to slavery. For Black people, moving about freely was not a right afforded to them, which is something in today's world called "driving while Black"—all gut wrenching and restrictive to this today.

My grandfather Robert "Bob" Coleman came to New Jersey from Danville, Virginia, in the 1950s to visit his grandfather's unmarried sister. He decided to stay with his great-aunt in the same house on Columbia Avenue that he later owned. Bob had no intention of staying in New Jersey, but someone told him that work was slow back home and that he may get a job at the Otto Kaufman Farm in Skillman, New Jersey. He took the job, which led to another employment opportunity for Reed's burial vault and septic tank service, where he worked for three years. They asked him to join the firm, which he did and stayed for fourteen years. Bob admitted it was hard work, but he liked it. He was asked to train someone, which he did; soon the owner was giving the trainee all the overtime. When Bob questioned the owner about it, he just shrugged his shoulders.

Sharecropping, farming and handyman skills had led my grandfather to be a jack-of-all trades, which exposed him to many opportunities to become a self-made, self-sufficient entrepreneur. He operated his own burial vault–making business with his partner, Henry Hodnett, a local African American man with deep family roots in the Hopewell area.

When Bob's great-aunt passed away, his uncle, who was affectionately called "Uncie," was also in poor health. Uncie owned the home on Columbia Avenue, and Bob stayed on to take care of him. While here, he also married my grandmother Queen Hester, whom he knew from Danville, in Pittsylvania County, Virginia. She had also come to New Jersey to help take care of Uncie. His wife, Cornelia, also known as "Auntie," had died at home at age eighty-eight; they had no children, so my grandparents worked as hard as they could to keep the homestead going while tending to the needs of Uncie.

Uncle Caleb signified that he would like to see my grandparents own his home. They weren't sure how to go about purchasing a home. Hester worked one day a week for the Smiths, a local White family in Hopewell. She was advised by the Smiths to write a letter making the estate an offer of terms. My grandparents offered cash, but actually had none—they had nothing to offer. With lots of determination and hard work and help from faithful friends lending them money, they were able to purchase the home that so many other folks from the community had their eye on. Uncie had lots of visitors toward the end of his life, but Grandpop knew they were really checking on how fast he was fading. He was ninety-eight years old by that time he died at home in 1954. Uncie was our connection to the famed baseball great Roy Campenella.

Caleb and Cornelia Womack, residents of Hopewell Borough, circa 1940s. *Author's collection.*

One evening when everyone was gathered around visiting Uncie, Grandpop and Grandmom told everyone they were going to a doctor appointment, but they really went to see Mr. Smith at the local bank and got a loan to buy the house, which Grandpop was proud to say they paid off in four years. After that loan was paid off, they thought they would get another loan to renovate the house. Years of neglect had taken a toll on the newly purchased home, so they decided in the early 1950s to apply for a loan to renovate their home. The local bank turned them down. Bob and Hester were both puzzled and disappointed by the negative response to their request. Finally, a friend recommended the Howard Savings Bank in Newark, New Jersey. Their representative was willing to give them a loan; a week later they were able to refinance their home, thus was our family's journey to homeownership in the borough of Hopewell.[101]

Robert Coleman receives Good Samaritan Award in Hopewell Borough, circa 1970s. *Author's collection.*

I've always had great admiration for my family and vividly remember an insult directed at my grandfather that I received when I was a teenager in the 1960s. I went to a local high-end dress shop, where I had helped my grandfather sand and refinish the hardwood floors. I saw all the beautiful clothes and went back there when it was open for business to buy an outfit I had seen while working. The store owner, a very well-dressed, stylish White woman approached me when I came in the door. At first I got that "What in the world are you doing in here look," so I immediately explained to her that I had seen an outfit that I wanted to purchase when I was helping my grandfather refinish her floors and told her his name. It was then she replied, "Oh yes, he's a nice boy," and also then that I gave her one of my looks and replied, "He's not a boy, he's my grandfather!" From that moment I realized the insult by this woman of privilege and that she would not get one dime of my hard-earned money. I went out of the door without the outfit I really wanted—and I never went back. I could not fathom the fact that she called my hardworking, handsome, well-built, highly respected, six-foot-five praying man (often mistaken for a pastor), extremely humble servant of the Lord who was always known as a loving husband and father—my grandfather—a "boy."

That paternalistic attitude of the supposedly dominant class didn't fly with me—this was the 1960s. A change had come in the way Black people were being viewed, the way we were being treated, and I was on board. These occurrences molded me for my civil rights crusade. As a young teenager, I was horrified watching my African American brothers and sisters actively protesting for change while being beaten, attacked and mauled by vicious dogs and killed by White mobs and police officers. These events ignited my interest in making a much-needed change—a social revolution.

As a group, we would gather after school to read the writings of African Americans like Langston Hughes, an American poet, activist, playwright and columnist. We learned about novelist, poet, playwright James Baldwin, writer of *Notes of a Native Son*, addressing social and racial issues of being Black in America. We read *I Know Why the Caged Bird Sings* by American author, screenwriter, actress, dancer, poet and civil rights activist Maya Angelou. *The Autobiography of Malcolm X* by Alex Haley and *Manchild in The Promised Land* by Claude Brown and *A Raisin in the Sun* by Lorraine Hansberry, just to mention a few writings, essays, poems, novels and literature that significantly changed my life living in my dark skin.

Now That I Know What I Know...

The Black experience in America left some so deeply scarred that some are unwilling to talk about it—the wounds are too deep. I myself find it difficult to research what my ancestors endured without feeling an overwhelming sadness. The struggles are real and ongoing into today's society. The effects of White privilege have left Black people stripped of landownership, generational wealth, most things essential in order to live productive, holistic lives.

An honest investigation of the enslaved population in my community has left me with many unanswered open-ended questions. Yes, we truly were "property" listed in White family wills along with the cattle, farm equipment and furniture. Clearly evident when we find our ancestors listed as "negro boy," "negro girl," "negro wench," "negro Richard" (referring to the Right Reverend Richard Allen, founder of the African Methodist Episcopal Church, AME) or "Negro Dick" (referring to an African American Revolutionary War veteran) is that we weren't considered important enough be named properly. The experience of scouring for countless hours looking for any detail of the presence and accomplishments of Blacks in this region made me realize that I was finding tidbits of information recorded through the lens of White historians. In the context of American history, we have tried to focus on the need to make room for these long-neglected stories.

What I will do is continue to use my pen to express my feelings about race relations in this country, to continue to speak up about intolerance and injustice. I will continue to read to educate myself. I will encourage diversity, continue to research and preserve Black history. I will not hide these truths in order to alleviate White guilt as I unearth America's venomous, racist past in our communities and in our nation. I will not be made to feel inferior. My grandmother Queen Hester Coleman repeatedly told me, "You are no better than anybody, but you are no less than anybody." I am on a mission for equal justice.

Growing up naïve, ignorant and oblivious to the social inequity in our country regarding people of color and the impact of the words I was memorizing daily as we collectively recited the Preamble and Pledge of Allegiance at Hopewell Elementary School during the 1960s still left me feeling disconnected. I didn't feel like "all men were equal." I learned that I was different—my hair was kinky, my skin was chocolate brown, my lips were puffy and pouty and those of the children and teachers around were not.

As a teenager, one thing I knew was that I was unashamedly Black. I was proud of the skin I am in. When I first heard Nina Simone singing "To Be Young, Gifted and Black" and Sonny Charles and the Checkmates singing "Black Pearl, Precious Little Girl," I was beaming with pride. They were singing about me.

Intertwining these vivid accounts of minorities and majorities living in two different worlds leads me to encourage us to join together as individuals to study, to change these primitive structures of systemic racism, to promote racial healing, education and community awareness. Highlighting our many ethnic differences while celebrating our need to coexist, we hopefully will be inspired to speak up and reshape the society we live in.

Living under oppressive conditions, navigating through life filled with inequality and injustices forced upon us, has empowered me to embrace our culture. Legends, oral histories, traditions and historical experiences help us weave our story of how chattel slavery contributed to the economic success of these wealthy communities.

We are no longer interested in continuing the narrative of not being interested in disguising and undermining the subject. These are shining examples of history as seen through the eyes of someone who viewed themselves as the dominant race, someone having no other frame of reference when telling African American history. White privilege is deep-seeded, as is the practice of demoralizing people of color.

When I read books, particularly historical accounts of someone of African descent, I will look at the hidden meaning behind the writing and read history critically. More importantly, I will continue to encourage everyone to be the change they want to see.

I recount my story for a couple reasons, but mostly to give context to what an African American family, my family, went through to be part of the American dream. In speaking with a longtime friend, Randy Hobler, he said, "While slavery has been abolished, the chains on our society are still there and we still are trying to move forward."

I am aware of the way African American history is portrayed in documents, literature, history books and stories—particularly those written through a White perspective. I am aware that the degradation of the Black race came from White America and how the campaign to characterize us as buffoons, stupid, lazy, slothful, over-sexed, beastly or subhuman has been a deliberate idealogue with origins in White supremacy dating back centuries.

In *Hopewell Heritage*, I read a chapter titled "The Hopewell Great Day in 1825," which commemorated the Declaration of Independence on July 4, 1825. It was about Hopewell, the town I have lived in all of my life. It has been said that the event was one of the greatest Hopewell has ever witnessed, with thousands of people in attendance to hear speeches, eat, drink and come dressed in their very finest. In this chapter, one of the stories mentioned was about an African American man named Frank Baragern with an ox and a cart. Lewis noted that

> *Frank Baragern, a black man, was responsible for making a great deal of sport for the boys. He drove a single ox harnessed like a horse to a small cart. As soon as he put in an appearance, the boys would commence to shout, "There he comes," and this was the signal for all to run and meet the art and ox. Perhaps forty would meet him beyond the village and someone would commence to hallo like a "jackmule" or like an ox in the throes of death. The ox would then erect his tail, put down his head and give a loud bawl, and away he would go, without paying any attention to Frank's plea of "whoa, whoa, whoa." No wonder the boys would follow in the rear and make all sorts of noises and generally by the time he arrived at the center of town, the cart would be overturned. The driver would be in the ditch, or perhaps chasing the ox down the road, until he was stopped by someone along the roadside. When caught the boys would help him rig up another race and this would be kept up until they were tired of the sport, or Frank got as much whisky as he wanted and left for home.*[102]

How a race of people is portrayed can have a lasting impression on a child, which includes me. I remember "Carnival Time" in Hopewell in the 1960s while I watched a Black man at the carnival sitting on a plank in a dunking booth waiting for someone to throw balls at him, hoping to hit the target so that he would plunge into the water. There would be long lines of White folks waiting to pitch the balls—there was a net around the booth to protect the person being dunked. I knew something was not right about this game. As an adult, I found out that it was not uncommon to see the "African Dip," "Dunk the Nigger," "Hit the Coon" or, most appalling and extremely offensive, "Hit the Nigger Baby" games, which were especially popular at traveling carnival shows, seashore resorts and fairgrounds across the United States.

Never in my wildest dreams did I realize the ever-recognizable jingle of the ice cream truck came from words written by actor Harry C. Browne. The racist song titled "Nigger Love a Watermelon Ha! Ha! Ha!" was released in March 1916 by Columbia Records. (Not all ice cream trucks play this same song, but a great many of them do.) Songs such as these were commonly used in Blackface minstrel shows. The words to an ice cream jingle song are:

> *Nigger love a watermelon ha ha ha!*
> *Nigger love a watermelon ha ha ha!*
> *For here, they're made with a half a pound of co'l*
> *There's nothing like a watermelon for a hungry coon*[103]

Now when I hear that jingle of an ice cream truck and see children scrambling to the window, I wonder what people would think if they knew the words to that catchy jingle. With a new understanding, I now know it's up to me to inform them because it has literally tainted the fun of hearing the jingle of an ice cream truck and the memory of my children when they heard the truck coming.

My memory of picking out a ripe sugar baby watermelon with Grandpop from his highly treasured backyard garden has also been tainted—even though it's a memory that always gave me pure joy. I can still see him give the melon a nice "thump" to be sure it was ripe enough before he sliced his butcher knife through it to cut it in half, sprinkle it with salt and, with big smiles, watch as we enjoyed our homegrown delectable treat. My family has always enjoyed watermelon, especially after a long day of working in the hot sun weeding and tilling our garden, most likely a tradition passed down through their years of toiling in the cotton and tobacco fields in Virginia.

For these sweet, sacred memories of something so pure and honest to be poisoned by derogatory racist stereotypes designed to defame and belittle people of color is unconscionable. I'm proud that I have always had a healthy view of myself as an African American woman; however, two decades later as a researcher, I refuse to spend a nanosecond of my time or energy on a system designed to exploit or make me feel inferior. I will never again be made to feel like an outsider in my own country because of the color of my skin. Most importantly, I will not pass this feeling of shame on to my children or grandchildren.

Since researching for my first book, *If These Stones Could Talk*, my thoughts on race and the long legacy of the African American struggle have opened my eyes to a new way I look at the way history has, or has not, been taught. My commitment as a tenacious activist for change has grown more than ever, telling the stories of my country and my community, to begin healing through promoting and raising awareness of our *true* American history, fostering conversations that will move us toward a better understanding of who we are as a people and a nation.

As people of color, we are walking reminders of the real truth of racism in our country. Dr. Michael E. Dyson, professor of African American studies, stated, "Avoiding White discomfort continues to leave us ignorant. You can't just ask White brothers and sisters who have been participants in a particular problem of oppression, how to relieve it. Ask the people who have been victims of it. Discomfort is a crucial tool to make people learn."[104]

19

THE VOICE OF BEVERLY MILLS

REFLECTIONS OF A BLACK WOMAN NAVIGATING THROUGH A WHITE WORLD

It can be a sobering thought when you come to the realization there are more years behind you than ahead. As I watch the years fly by, it seems reflection is my go-to pastime, along with early bedtimes and easily digestible foods. But this is in no way an indictment on aging, not in the least. It is a testament to living, with a semblance of sanity, in a country that has done its best to erase what it has been treated as my "offensive" Blackness and to minimize the legacy of my African American people.

I've struggled to find words to share my personal thoughts with you—the reader—as we close out our book *African Americans of Central New Jersey: A History of Harmony and Hostility*. I have feared that what we hoped would be our readers' takeaway will be drowned out by my words of sadness, despair and anger.

When I started this journey with my good friend and colleague Elaine Buck in 2016, there was no way we could brace ourselves for what we were about to uncover. Each day, month and year, the layers began to unravel and reveal to us a bank of information that we could never have imagined. There were many times that we simply had to stop reading what we had found in order to collect ourselves. Several times I simply broke down, unable to continue on. Elaine and I have been proud of the education we received as graduates of one of the top school systems in the state of New Jersey, but most of the information we have uncovered was never included—or remotely alluded to—in our school curriculum. Instead, we were taught a more convenient, less caustic *version* of so-called American history, in which all the cancerous parts had been removed so the story would appear healthy. American history narration has purposefully eliminated essential critical contributions of the enslaved who—with their free labor—created one of the most powerful nations on earth, one community at a time, starting with the lash of a whip. So, as we began to fill in the blank pieces of this centuries-old puzzle, a more authentic picture started to come into view—and the authenticity isn't pretty. No wonder those who had the power to cover up parts of this picture took every opportunity to do so.

Growing up as a Black female in a predominately White town intimidated, suffocated, discouraged and bruised me. However, it also elevated, toughened, emboldened and compelled me to aspire to more than the supposed inherent limitations associated with Blackness.

While in elementary school, a few White female classmates and I became friendly—relationships that endure to the present day. But it wasn't until a few years ago that one of my friends shared a story about the difficulty she experienced just from bringing a Black child into her sweet White suburban home. My offending Blackness had proven to be too much for a White mother in the early 1960s, so much so that she sought advice from older female family members about how to handle the "situation." The advice this mother got was to discourage the friendship between my friend and me since I *may* have an older brother that could become interested in my young White friend. In spite of it all, however, we continued to be friends. Eventually, my friend's parents came to accept my offending Blackness and even extended a polite invitation.

Growing up on South Main Street in Pennington, New Jersey, on a block that I discovered began with my Blackwell/Smith ancestors, did not spare me from being acutely aware of the American caste system. My mother, like many of the other young Black mothers on the block, worked for local White families. My mother never learned to drive, so my mother and I would be picked up by whichever White woman my mother would be working for on a particular day. Since this was the early 1950s, off we would go for a day's work, in the back of the popular suburban car of that time—the station wagon. I did my best to entertain myself while my mother worked either by watching TV or playing with a White child who was home from school for whatever reason. It was common for my mother and me to be at work from morning into the midafternoon. My mother would prepare lunch and serve the lady of the house in the dining room. Then my mother and I would retreat to the kitchen to eat our lunch. So my education began before my first day of school; that we, my mother and I, were marginalized people.

As I got older, I felt the pressure to assimilate more to the surroundings in which I lived. Conquering my kinky hair was but one example of the hardships. The early 1960s also brought chemical hair straighteners to the market for Black women. It was a game-changer, and my uncle Herb, a salesman for a vendor who sold straighteners to Black hairdressers, supplied my grandmother, who owned a beauty salon. Referred to as "perms" for Black women, it was the absolute opposite of the White perm. Whereas the Black perm was designed to conquer offending kinky/curly hair, the White perm was to create curls and body to otherwise straight hair. So as my grandmother did her best to prepare me for the stinging and burning my scalp would endure, I endured the extreme discomfort in order to have straight hair. The result was achieved in spite of handfuls of once beautiful, thick hair that went swirling down the drain.

I talk about these aspects of my life to highlight the complexities of growing up in a White community and the need to conform to the social construct of "Whiteness." I watched my mother, father and grandparents navigate through this world in their own way—my father and grandfather leaning more toward subservience. This couldn't have been more evident than when I was nineteen and moved to New York City. My mother had passed away a year earlier, less than one month after she gave birth to my brother, my only sibling, who is eighteen years my junior. At that time, my mother, at forty years old, was seen as a high-risk pregnancy. She experienced an appendicitis attack in her fourth month of pregnancy from which she recovered. About three and a half months later, she delivered my brother, Travis, prematurely, but she never had the opportunity to hold him. Returning from the hospital, my mother continued to experience complications and was advised to consult the local White doctor, who treated her and the other local pregnant women. My mother's sister, Bonnie, had been concerned that this doctor was very casual and dismissive about my mother's care; never did he advise her to come to his office for an examination, nor did he offer to make a house call—which was still customary at that time. Instead, he simply suggested that she "rest" and keep her legs elevated to lessen the seemingly endless blood flow.

When my mother died from a blood clot that traveled to her lungs, three months shy of her forty-first birthday, my exposure to the insidiousness of Whiteness came more sharply into view. Would my mother had survived if her Blackness had not influenced the doctor's view of the type of care she should receive? It is highly doubtful that a local White woman would have received such casual attention. But if my father was angry at the local White doctor, he never said so—but I know I was angry.

I had always been an observer of the way my father and grandfather interacted with the local White folk—people they regarded as their friends though I never saw any formal socializing. Yet for my father and grandfather, Pennington was always home—except for my father's service in a segregated army unit during World War II. My father and grandfather's conservative views always mirrored those of the local White folks. In the early 1960s, my grandfather Alfonso declared Dr. Martin Luther King Jr. to be nothing but a troublemaker and rabble-rouser. That my father was silent on the subject, never expressing an opinion, to me, spoke volumes. The assassination of King seemed inconsequential to my father and grandfather. However, family members who lived outside of the Pennington "bubble" were outraged at my father and grandfather's views about race and Blackness. In fact, the passivity and evasiveness of these two men opened a bitter political divide within my family.

My evolution from chemically straightened hair to an afro dismayed not only my father and grandfather but also my hairdresser grandmother. Each time I came home for a visit, I was told that my appearance did not match my upbringing. And when I came home in African braids and a ring in my nose, they pretty much gave up! Perhaps their disgust was not such much about my appearance but what they could see taking place within me: a reexamination of who I was as a Black woman who had been groomed to fit within the carefully crafted race and class structure of America.

My purpose in sharing these stories is not to disparage my family or to make them appear ignorant or mean-spirited. They did their best to extract dignity and safety from a hostile environment. My intention is to illustrate the unseen damage that the construct of Whiteness can inflict on African American individuals, families and communities. Whiteness, systemic racism and its centuries-old predecessor—the caste system—have caused immeasurable harm to countless people. And even in the face of this relentless dehumanization, I am continuously amazed at the remarkable resilience of Black people. I cannot help but wonder, however, if my father and grandfather had lived to the twenty-first century, would they still hold the same belief system? How would they try to rationalize the countless Black people killed because the prevailing caste system has allowed this to happen time and time again without repercussions?

Since the 2016 election, America has experienced a proliferation of hate crimes, hate speech, White supremacy groups and the uprising of Americans dedicated to protecting the caste system. I wonder if this would cause my father or grandfather to have a moment of self-reflection if they were still living? Would they still remain comfortable being part of a caste system which "was to remain in its place like an ill-fitting suit that constantly must be altered, seams and darts re-sewn to fit the requirement of the upper caste, going back to the enslavers who resented displays of industriousness and intellect in the people they saw themselves as owning."[105]

More than a half century ago, I returned to Pennington to live after my three-year stay in New York. I have watched the town change from being strictly conservative to mostly liberal. In 2016, I had the honor of being Pennington's first African American woman to be elected to the borough council. Since 2006, when my coauthor, Elaine Buck, first received that phone call from Walter Niemeier in West Amwell, asking for our help with saving an old burial ground, I have been devoted to uncovering and telling the African American story. It was a life-changing call that became the catalyst for us to begin our research for our first book, *If These Stones Could Talk*. Throughout the years, we have spoken before thousands of people, to tell our story and to educate those who wanted to learn more about the African American narrative of the real people we knew and to whom we are related and descended. Elaine and I have been told our stories are compelling and that the history we uncover is eye-opening because much we present has been hidden in plain sight. We feel honored to be the ambassadors and spotlight holders to illuminate this truth.

It is my hope that after reading this book, our work has moved you to look differently as some of the beliefs you may have held onto during your life. We wanted this book to take a closer look at the building of community and who these people were who came before us to make it all possible. We wanted to tell you the stories of Black people who had their own personal dreams, goals, strengths, limitations and hopes—the same as their White brethren. There were times when I struggled with writing this book, as it is a past and a present story. But I also see it as a story about how Black loyalty may not always be reciprocated but how Black agency can be, and always has been, attainable in some form—even if you don't believe it to be so.

YES, WE REMAIN HOPEFUL

Since the 2018 release of our book *If These Stones Could Talk*, White readers have reached out to us to share disturbing family secrets that had not been talked about for years. Some of these people talked about how they felt compelled to do self-examination about their own attitudes about race, White privilege and how they became self-reflective in ways they had not expected. Some of those expressed such self-reflection; others were familiar with the region in other ways. What we heard was a wish that their ancestors—or even their younger *selves*—had behaved differently. Some felt mortified, ashamed and angry. Others, though, didn't express feelings one way or the other but just wanted to share a story. But those who clearly felt shame and embarrassment also conveyed a desire to do better in the hope of a better future for our communities and our country.

So, what would it look like to create that better future? We appreciate those who came forward with their stories as we continue to struggle, as Black women and members of our communities, to deal with the residual effects of hostility. What are some of the choices to turn anti-racism into a verb instead of a noun? Acknowledge the past, express your guilt and embarrassment but then put a plan in action to do something about it—contribute to an organization or cause that broadens the understanding of African American history or culture; maybe you could expand your social circle (are all your friends and acquaintances White?). Maybe you would support your school systems to teach African American history without restriction—in a curriculum that explores Black Americans contributions, victories *and* victimization. Can you educate yourself by reading literature written by African American authors? Can you remain alert to the hiring practices at your workplace and ask yourself if you're comfortable with the number of Black people in higher-wage and/or leadership positions? Can you add to the list of ways to start moving the needle to effect change?

This book was written with the intent to generate thoughts on how we, Black *and* White people, *all people*, can take action to ensure a better future. Today, in our world of White "wokeness," Black Lives Matter and the race to suppress what many believe to be critical race theory, we do not have a minute to rest. We ask that anyone struggling with a disturbing discovery in their family to turn their guilt and embarrassment into empowerment and use it to become a motivator for change.

African Americans are still recuperating from the past but remain hopeful for a brighter tomorrow. People like Walter Niemeier, a White man from a nearby community, gave us hope that inspired us to set our own journey into motion and to believe that we would have White allies on that journey. Walter was not content to be an observer of something he knew to be wrong. Instead, he decided to take a leadership role, despite threats from—and exclusion by some—members of his White community. By literally putting himself in harm's way, Walter remained steadfast to do his part to right what he knew to be a wrong. For this, we will always honor his memory.

It is our hope that after you have read *African Americans of Central New Jersey: A History of Harmony and Hostility*, you will be among those to ask, "What can *I* do now, and how can *I* contribute toward a better future for our country?"

Our advice to you is to let your leadership shine the light! Be a change agent!

Peace and blessings,
Beverly and Elaine

NOTES

Foreword

1. Dolores Hayden, *The Power of Place: Urban Landscapes as Public History* (Cambridge, MA: MIT Press, 1995).
2. Roy Rosenzweig and David Thelen, *The Presence of the Past: Popular Uses of History in American Life* (New York: Columbia University Press, 1998).

1. White and Black Communities Grow Side by Side but Not Together

3. James J. Gigantino II, *The Ragged Road to Abolition Slavery and Freedom in New Jersey, 1775–1865* (Philadelphia: University of Pennsylvania Press, 2016), 95.
4. Henry Scofield Cooley, *A Study of Slavery in New Jersey* (Baltimore: Johns Hopkins Press), 31.
5. Ibid.
6. Ibid.
7. "Sourland Mountain Settlers and Their Descendants." An ongoing study in 1984 of Rock Mill family surname listings conducted by Roxanne Carkhuff of the Hunterdon Genealogical Services.
8. Cooley, *Study of Slavery*, 26–27.

9. W.O. Blake, *The History of Slavery and the Slave Trade* (Columbus, OH: 1869), chapter 10, "African Slave Trade in the Eighteenth Century—The Middle Passage," 126–28.

10. Cooley, *Study of Slavery*, 11.

11. "The 1619 Project," *New York Times Magazine*, August 18, 2019, 17.

12. The Town Records of Hopewell, New Jersey, New Jersey Society of the Colonial Dames of America, 1931.

13. Derrick Ramon Spires, *The Practice of Citizenship: Black Politics and Print Culture in the Early United States*, (Philadelphia: University Pennsylvania Press, 2019); Rosalind Williams, *The Letters of Captain Paul Cuffee* (Washington, D.C.: Howard University Press), 1996.

14. Michael Barga, "Free African Society (Founded 1780)," Social Welfare History Project, https://socialwelfare.library.vcu.edu/religious/african-union-society/.

15. Carol V.R. George, *Segregated Sabbaths, Richard Allen and the Rose of Independent Black Churches 1760–1840* (New York: New York University Press, 1973), 54–55.

16. Felix Brenton, "American Colonization Society (1816–1964)," *BlackPast*, https://www.blackpast.org/african-american-history/american-colonization-society-1816-1964/.

17. *Princeton Seminary and Slavery: A Report of the Historical Audit Committee* (Princeton, NJ: Princeton University Press, 2018), https://slavery.ptsem.edu/wp-content/uploads/2019/10/Princeton-Seminary-and-Slavery-Report-rev10-19.pdf.

18. Ibid.

19. Simon Webb, *The Life and Times of Paul Cuffe, Black Quaker Abolitionist* (Langley Press, 2020), 11.

20. Craig Hollander, "Princeton and the Colonization Movement," https://slavery.princeton.edu/stories/princeton-and-the-colonization-Movement.

21. Ibid.

22. Margaret J. O'Connell, *Pennington Profile: A Capsule of State and Nation* (Pennington, NJ: Pennington Library, 1966), 19.

23. Richard Allen, "The Life, Experience, and Gospel Labours of the Rt. Rev. Richard Allen," Documenting the American South, https://docsouth.unc.edu/neh/allen/allen.html.

24. M. Goodspeed, "The Story of Little Jim," *Goodspeed Histories, New Jersey History and Genealogy*, August 4, 2017, https://goodspeedhistories.com/the-story-of-little-jim/.

2. Light on Hidden Hopewell Stories

25. Historical Sketch of Hopewell Centennial Speech, July 4, 1876, https://hopewellhistoryproject.org.
26. Ralph Ege, *Pioneers of Old Hopewell* (Hopewell, NJ: Race & Savidge, 1908), 122.
27. C.W. Larison, MD, *Silvia Dubois: A Biografy of the Slav Who Whipt Her Mistres and Ganed Her Fredom* (New York: Oxford University Press, 1988), 60–61.
28. Cooley, *Study of Slavery*, 39.
29. "Matters of Local Interest," *Somerset (NJ) Unionist*, March 13, 1873.
30. Ibid.
31. Graham Hodges, *Black New Jersey: 1664 to the Present Day* (Newark, NJ: Rutgers University Press, 2019), 31.
32. Witness Stones Project, www.witnessstonesproject.org.
33. Ibid.
34. Alice Blackwell Lewis, "Hamlets and Towns Not Included in Other Stories," in *Hopewell Valley Heritage* (Trenton, NJ: Parker Printing, 1973), 163–64.
35. Ibid., 163.
36. Ege, *Pioneers of Old Hopewell*, 122, 125.
37. Ibid.
38. T.J. Luce, *New Jersey's Sourland Mountain* (Neshanic Station, NJ: Sourland Planning Council, 2001), 84.
39. M. Goodspeed, "Little Jim, Part Three," *Goodspeed Histories, New Jersey History and Genealogy*, August 18, 2017, https://goodspeedhistories.com/little-jim-part-three/.

3. White and Black Blackwells Grow Their Legacies

40. Hopewell Township Historic Preservation Commission, National Register of Historic Places, 1995.
41. Find a Grave, "Capt Joab Houghton," https://www.findagrave.com/memorial/9607231/joab.
42. Alice Blackwell Lewis, "Of Other Hamlets and Towns," in *Hopewell Valley Heritage* (Trenton, NJ: Parker Printing, 1973), 163.
43. Harry J. Podmore, *Trenton Old and New* (Trenton, NJ: MacCrelish & Quigley Company, 1964), https://www.trentonhistory.org/Old&New.html#THEUNITEDSTATESHOTEL.

44. Ibid.

45. Historical Currency Converter, historicalstatistics.org.

46. Cooley, *Study of Slavery*, 47.

47. Ibid., 27.

48. Hunterdon County Court of Common Pleas, Manumission of Nancy Blackwell, April 9, 1827.

49. Henry Louis Gates Jr., "Did Black People Own Slaves?" American Renaissance, March 4, 2013, https://www.amren.com/news/2013/03/did-black-people-own-slaves/.

50. Larry Koger, *Black Slaveowners: Free Black Slave Masters in South Carolina, 1790–1860* (Jefferson, NC: McFarland, 1985).

51. Will and Probate of Enoch Drake 1822, Hunterdon County Probate No. 3180, NJSA.

52. David Blackwell, "Frost Blackwell and His Family," unpublished manuscript prepared by a descendant of the Blackwell family, January 2008.

53. Ibid.

4. Oliver Hart and Friday Truehart Bring Their Lives to Hopewell Borough

54. Robert Andrew Baker, Paul J. Craven and R. Marshall Blalock, *History of the First Baptist Church of Charleston, South Carolina, 1682–2007*, 325th Anniversary Edition (Springfield, MO: Particular Baptists Press, 2007), 123–24.

55. Ibid., 137–38.

56. Diary of Reverend Oliver Hart, South Carolina Library, Oliver Hart Papers, 1741–1795.

57. Cooley, *Study of Slavery*, 30.

58. Baker and Craven, "History of the First Baptist Church," 130.

59. Diary of Reverend Oliver Hart.

60. Ibid.

61. Alice Blackwell Lewis, "About the Hart Family," in *Hopewell Valley Heritage* (Trenton, NJ: Parker Printing, 1973), 69.

62. According to the Old Testament, Isaac was a "miracle child" born to Abraham and Sarah when they were beyond childbearing age, and through him God promised to protect Abraham's lineage; brothers Aaron and Moses were God's designees to lead slaves out of bondage (Exodus).

63. Hunterdon County Book of Deeds, Book 30, 275.
64. Hunterdon County Book of Deeds, No. 254, 272.

5. Looking Backward: White Blackwells, Black Trueharts

65. Lewis, "About the Hart Family," 69.
66. "Old Billy Truehart Loved Home, Defied Lindbergh," *Baltimore Afro-American*, March 28, 1930, 4.
67. Ibid.
68. Lewis, "About the Hart Family," 69.

6. The White and Black Blew Families

69. *Hopewell Valley Historical Society Newsletter* (Late Winter/Spring 2017): 835–38.
70. Ibid.
71. Ibid.
72. University of Minnesota Human Rights Library, http://hrlibrary.umn.edu.
73. "NJ Women Vote: The 19th Amendment at 100," New Brunswick Free Public Library, Women's History Virtual Tour Project (project to share diverse stories of women in New Jersey at five sites along the NJ Women's Heritage Trail), https://www.nbfpl.org/suffrage.

8. Pennington's Black Community Sinks Deeper Roots

74. Alice Blackwell Lewis, "The Titus Family," in *Hopewell Valley Heritage* (Trenton, NJ: Parker Printing, 1973), 262.
75. Ibid.
76. Ibid.
77. "The Fugitive Slave Law of 1850," *Bill of Rights in Action* 34, no. 2 (Winter 2019): 5–6. https://www.crf-usa.org/images/pdf/Fugitive-Slave-Law-1850.pdf.

9. Two Blocks Away, but Worlds Apart

78. "William P. Howe," *Hopewell Valley Historical Society Newsletter* 31, no. 2 (Fall 2012): 681.

79. Estimated Size of Puerto Rican Community in Various New Jersey Cities, 1955, https://trentonlib.org/wp-content/uploads/2020/08/Historical-Report-about-Puerto-Ricans-in-New-Jersey-from-1955.pdf.

80. Ibid., 13.

81. Letter from the First Baptist Church of Pennington to the Howe family, submitted by Louella Richardson, church secretary, on behalf of H. Lewis, minister, and the church body.

11. Looking Backward: Darlis Maksymovich

82. Last Will and Testament of Muscoe Boulware (1758–1825).

12. The Pennington Seminary: An Anchor of "Community"

83. Rachel L. Warns, "272 Slaves Were Sold to Save Georgetown. What Does It Owe Their Descendants?" *New York Times*, April 17, 2016, https://www.nytimes.com/2016/04/17/us/georgetown-university-search-for-slave-descendants.html.

84. The Pennington School, "Our History of Inclusion," https://www.pennington.org/admission/new-history

85. Ibid.

86. Kenneth C. Anderson, "The History of The Pennington School," February 1968. This is a 168-page typescript donated to the Pennington School by Kenneth C. Anderson, class of 1939, Fairfax, Virginia.

87. *Princeton Recollector* 1, no. 4 (October 1975).

14. Looking Backward: Meghan Speaks at Her December 20, 2020 Interview

88. James J. Gigantino II, *The Ragged Road to Abolition Slavery and Freedom in New Jersey, 1775–1865* (Philadelphia: University of Pennsylvania Press, 2016), 97.

16. Henry Ballard Clark: A Seventh Son Migrates from Virginia

89. Henry Louis Gates, *Stony the Road: Reconstruction, White Supremacy, and the Rise of Jim Crow* (New York: Penguin Press, 2019), 9.
90. Ibid., 36.
91. Mercer County, "Beginning of an Industrial Giant," https://www.mercercounty.org/community/history/beginning-of-an-industrial-giant.
92. *Trenton Times*, March 6, 1904.
93. Margaret J. O'Connell, *Pennington Profile*, 1st ed (Self-published, 1966), 160–61.

17. A Castle Built on Hate…and a Grave of a Civil Rights Icon

94. Diccon Hyatt, "The Secrets of Hopewell's Castle Revealed," Community News, May 1, 2019, https://www.communitynews.org/towns/hopewell-express/the-secrets-of-hopewell-s-castle-revealed/article__bcc957cd-1226-5d3d-a55d-497b13c1bb3c.html.
95. Ibid.
96. Ibid.
97. Hyatt, "Secrets of Hopewell's Castle."
98. D. Hevesi, D. "William Ashby, Longtime Worker for Civil Rights, Is Dead at 101," *New York Times*, May 19, 1991, https://www.nytimes.com/1991/05/19/obituaries/william-ashby-longtime-worker-for-civil-rights-is-dead-at-101.html.
99. David M. Kidd, "'History Written with Lightning': Religion, White Supremacy, and the Rise and Fall of Thomas Dixon, Jr." (PhD dissertation, College of William and Mary, 2014), https://scholarworks.wm.edu/etd/1539623616/.
100. William M. Ashby Papers, Newark Library Collection, "Tales Without Hate," 46.

18. The Voice of Elaine Buck: Personal Reflections on Race and the Long Legacy of the African American Struggle

101. *Hopewell Valley News* 34, no. 5, February 2, 1989.
102. Alice Blackwell Lewis, *Hopewell Valley Heritage* (Trenton, NJ: Parker Printing, 1973), 102.

103. Theodore R. Johnson III, "Recall That Ice Cream Truck Song? We Have Unpleasant News For You," *Code Switch: Word Watch*, May 11, 2014, https://www.npr.org/sections/codeswitch/2014/05/11/310708342/recall-that-ice-cream-truck-song-we-have-unpleasant-news-for-you.
104. Michael Eric Dyson, *The View* (ABC-NYC), November 4, 2021.

19. The Voice of Beverly Mills: Reflections of a Black Woman Navigating Through a White World

105. Isabel Wilkerson, *Caste: The Origins of Our Discontents* (New York: Random House, 2020), 231.

ABOUT THE AUTHORS

BEVERLY MILLS is a cofounder of the Stoutsburg Sourland African American Museum and coauthor of *If These Stones Could Talk*. Beverly proudly received the Kirkus Book Review in October 2018 and in 2019 the New Jersey Author's Award Non-fiction Popular Works Category presented by the NJ Studies Academic Alliance by the History and Preservation Section of the NJ Library Association and the Special Collections Archives at Rutgers University. In 2020, Beverly partnered with the Museum of the American Revolution on identifying potential 1801 Montgomery Township, New Jersey African American and female voters for their exhibition titled *When Women Lost the Vote*. On December 23, 2020, Beverly was featured in the *New York Times* in an article titled "Helping the Stones Talk: Recovering Black History." This story also appeared in the online *Smithsonian Magazine* on December 24, 2020, and in the *Chicago Tribune* on December 26, 2020, under the title "Uncovering Lost Black History Stone by Stone." For Black History Month, Beverly was interviewed by veteran journalist Pat Battle for an NBC (Channel 4, NYC) segment titled, "Uncovering Mercer County's Forgotten Past." Beverly also appeared in a Black History month interview with Crystal Cranmore, "Unearthing Black Contributions in New Jersey" for ABC (Channel 7, NYC). In 2021, Beverly received the Doris C. Carpenter Award on behalf of Preservation New Jersey for her work on the March of America's Diverse Army through New Jersey and the Solomon Northup Family Award for uplifting the memory of enslaved people. In June 2022, Beverly Mills appeared in the New Jersey PBS Special titled *The Price of Silence, The Forgotten Story of New Jersey's Enslaved People*, produced by Truehart Productions.

SHARON ELAINE BUCK, who prefers Elaine, is a founder the Stoutsburg Sourland African American Museum. As coauthor of *If These Stones Could Talk*, Elaine proudly received the Kirkus Book Review in October 2018 and in 2019 the New Jersey Author's Award Non-fiction Popular Works Category presented by the NJ Studies Academic Alliance by the History and Preservation Section of the NJ Library Association and the Special Collections Archives at Rutgers University. In 2020, Elaine partnered with the Museum of the American Revolution on identifying potential 1801 Montgomery Township African American and female voters for the exhibition titled *When Women Lost the Vote*. On December 23, 2020, Elaine was also featured in the *New York Times* in "Helping the Stones Talk: Recovering Black History." This story also appeared in the online *Smithsonian Magazine* on December 24, 2020, and in the *Chicago Tribune* on December 26, 2020, under the title "Uncovering Lost Black History Stone by Stone." For Black History Month, Elaine was interviewed by veteran journalist Pat Battle for an NBC (Channel 4, NYC) segment titled "Uncovering Mercer County's Forgotten Past." Elaine also appeared in a Black History month interview with Crystal Cranmore, "Unearthing Black Contributions in New Jersey," for ABC (Channel 7, NYC). In 2021, Elaine received the Doris C. Carpenter Award on behalf of Preservation New Jersey for her work on the March of America's Diverse Army through New Jersey and the Solomon Northup Family Award for uplifting the memory of enslaved people. In June 2022, Elaine Buck appeared in the New Jersey PBS Special titled *The Price of Silence, The Forgotten Story of New Jersey's Enslaved People*, produced by Truehart Productions.

Visit us at
www.historypress.com
....